DISCOVERING HISTORY

EXPANSION, TRADE AND INDUSTRY

ROS ADAMS

Series Editors
NEIL TONGE &
PETER HEPPLEWHITE

Causeway Press Ltd

To Doris, Chuck, Rene and Bill.

Acknowledgement

With thanks to Steve Lancaster for all his help and support and also to Roy Gower, Ian Fisher and the staff of Sandringham School.

Ros Adams
October, 1992

Note to teachers

1. **The Focus pages**
   Each chapter contains a Focus page which aims to engage the reader, excite curiosity and raise issues. All Focus pages are based on primary source material.

2. **The Sources**
   Most of the written sources are taken from original documents. The language has been adapted to aid comprehension.

   All original artwork is based on primary source material - either literary, pictorial or archaeological.

3. **The Teachers' Guide**
   A teachers' guide is available. It is photocopiable and provides assessment tests, guidance for marking, advice for teaching, additional information and worksheets with further activities including games and simulations.

CONTENTS

1 INTRODUCTION

Live pictures from war-torn parts of the world appear on our television screens almost daily. Until the mid 19th century people in Britain received news of battles weeks or even months after the event. Their view of the fighting came from official reports written by army officers or from sketches or paintings made by artists who might not even have seen the battle themselves.

In 1854 Britain, France and Turkey went to war against Russia in the Crimea. The Crimean War was the first major European war for forty years. For the first time newspapers sent journalists to report directly from the battlefield. For the first time too, photographs (invented in 1839) showed people the harsh realities of war.

The sources on these pages are examples of the kind of evidence historians use to learn about a particular event or period. Different types of evidence show us different points of view.

Source A A map of the Crimean War

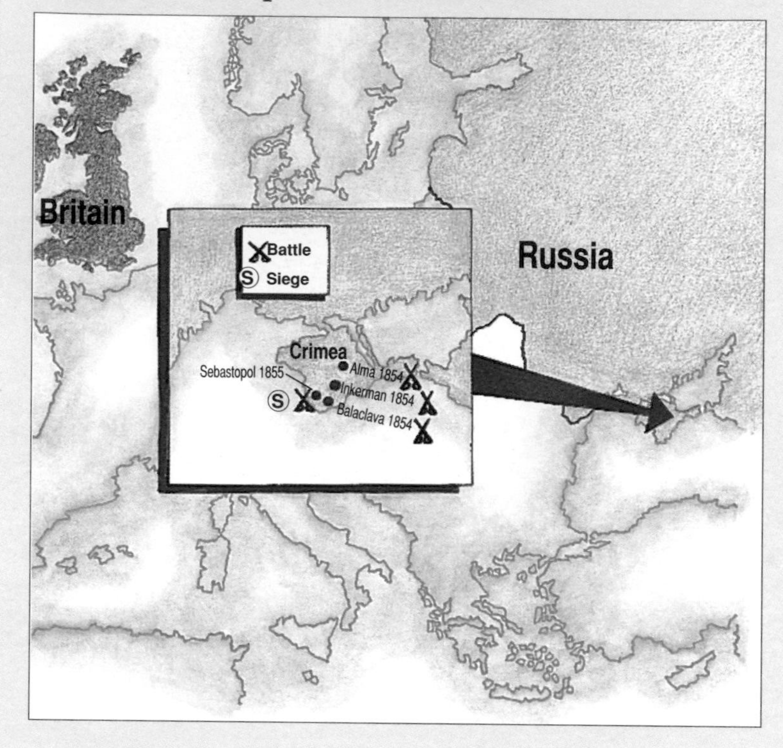

Source B Painting of the battle of the Alma

The Scots Fusilier Guards at the battle of the Alma on 20 September 1854. In the popular imagination the British troops were bold, heroic and almost unbeatable.

Source C Poetry

During the battle of Balaclava on 25 October 1854, the British cavalry commander misunderstood an order. As a result, 600 troops rode straight into Russian cannon fire. Fewer than 200 survived.

Storm'd at with shot and shell,
They that rode so well,
Rode thro' the jaws of death,
Half a league back again,
Up from the mouth of Hell,
All that was left of them,
Left of the six hundred.
Honour the brave and bold!
Long shall the tale be told,
Yea, when our babes are old
How they rode onward.

'The Charge of the Light Brigade', a poem by Alfred Lord Tennyson, 1855

Source D Newspapers

William Howard Russell was the first journalist to send reports straight from the front. His descriptions of the action were very popular with the British public.

At 1,200 yards the whole line of the enemy belched forth from thirty iron mouths, a flood of smoke and flame, through which flew the deadly balls. Their flight was marked by instant gaps in our ranks, by dead men and horses, by steeds running wounded or riderless across the plain. The first line was broken. It was joined by the second. They never halted or checked their speed an instant. They marched into the smoke and then were lost from view. The plain was strewn with their bodies and with the carcasses of horses. At twenty five to twelve not a British soldier, except the dead and dying, was left in front of these bloody Russian guns.

W. Russell's report of the charge of the Light Brigade, 'The Times', October 1854

Source E Photographs

A French 'cantinière' (refreshment carrier, a nursing assistant) helps a wounded soldier. Photographs like this showed the reality of war to people at home. Few had ever seen a battle.

Source F Modern reconstructions

A scene from the film 'The Charge of the Light Brigade' made in 1968.

Activities

1. a) Look at Sources A, B and C. What do they tell us about the Crimean war?
   b) Look at Sources D, E and F. Do they change your view of the war? How?
   c) What other sources would you want to see in order to build up a more accurate picture of the war?
2. How does Source D differ from war reports by modern journalists?
3. Look at Source F.
   a) If you were making a film about the Crimean war, which of Sources A to E would be helpful and why?
   b) What problems might you have making an accurate reconstruction of a battle like the one shown in Source F?

2 AGRICULTURE

New crops like oil seed rape are protected from disease by chemical sprays.

Themes

How many people do you know who work in farming? The answer will depend on where you live. In some areas of Britain a large proportion of the population still works in farming but overall less than 2% of the population does so.

In 1750 more than 70% of people farmed the land. Most were subsistence farmers – they grew just enough to feed themselves. Whole families worked together ploughing, sowing, weeding and harvesting the crops. This system had not changed very much for centuries.

By 1900 many changes had taken place in the countryside. These changes affected everything from the appearance of the land to the way it was farmed and who owned it. Some historians claim that the changes were so great that they amount to a revolution in agriculture.

This chapter looks at these questions.

- How and why did agriculture change?
- What impact did the changes have on the countryside?

Fields of cereal crops can be harvested in hours with combine harvesters.

Focus Activities

1. It is 1850. You have been given a job selling new machines to farmers who use the old farming methods. You invite farmers to a meeting.
   a) Make a presentation showing how farming techniques are changing and how these changes are improving farming.
   b) Some farmers are opposed to change. What arguments might they use and how would you reply to them?
   c) The new machines are expensive. Explain why it is worthwhile for farmers to buy them.
2. Study the pictures on both pages. Would you say that there has been progress in agriculture? Explain your answer.

Demands for higher productivity and profit have led to battery farming.

The changing countryside

Before the changes in agriculture, farmers relied on hand power or animal power. Inventions and the development of machinery meant a dramatic change in the way farmers worked. Machines saved time and labour. Farmers therefore had more time to make improvements – drainage ditches could be dug, fences built and fertilisers used to improve the soil. Changes in the ownership of land meant bigger farms and more specialisation. By 1900 many farmers lived off the profits made from selling their produce. They no longer simply grew food for themselves.

Before

Ploughing was slow, hard work.

In the summer everyone helped to gather the harvest. Crops were cut by hand, using a sickle.

After

Steam ploughs saved time and labour.

New machines meant greater efficiency and lower costs – fewer workers had to be paid.

The impact of enclosure

In 1700 perhaps as much as half the land in England and Wales (and all that in Scotland) was farmed using a system which had changed little since the Middle Ages – the 'open field' system.

The land around a village was divided into three (or more) fields. Each field was divided into strips. Farmers owned or rented separate strips in each field.

By 1700 this system had already begun to change. Land was enclosed – strips were joined together and surrounded by fences or hedges to form solid blocks that were farmed separately. This allowed specialisation. For example, in Kent fruit and hops were grown. In Devon, cider apples were the main crop. Enclosed farms were generally more productive than open fields.

In the second half of the 18th century enclosure became very widespread. By 1850 most of the farmland in England had been enclosed.

Source A The spread of enclosure

Most land enclosed by 1700

Districts most affected by Enclosure Acts

England as affected by Enclosure Acts

Number of Enclosure Acts 1760-1829

1760-69 : 385	1800-09 : 847
1770-79 : 660	1810-19 : 853
1780-89 : 246	1820-29 : 205
1790-99 : 469	

Source B The effects of enclosure

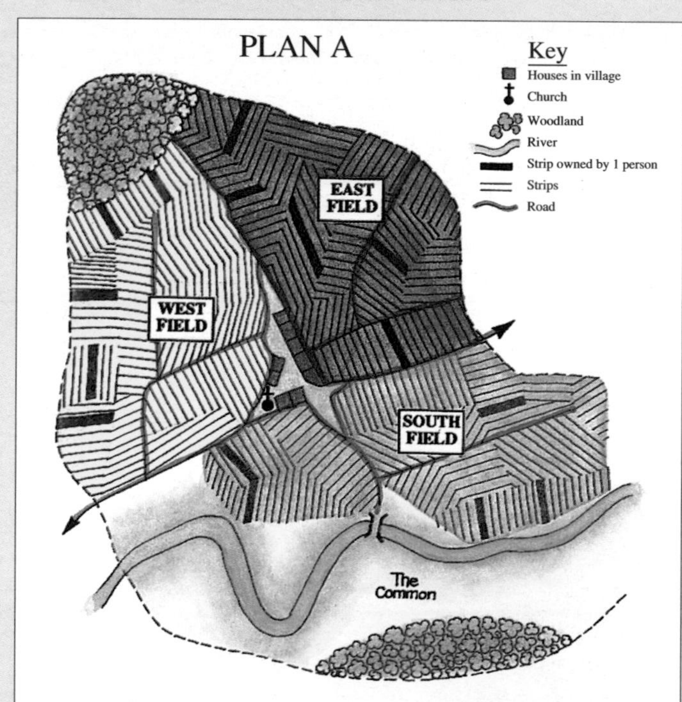

A village where land was farmed using the open field system. Every year, two of the fields would be sown with crops. The third field would be left 'fallow' (empty) to recover its fertility. Wood was cut from the woodland and animals grazed together on the common.

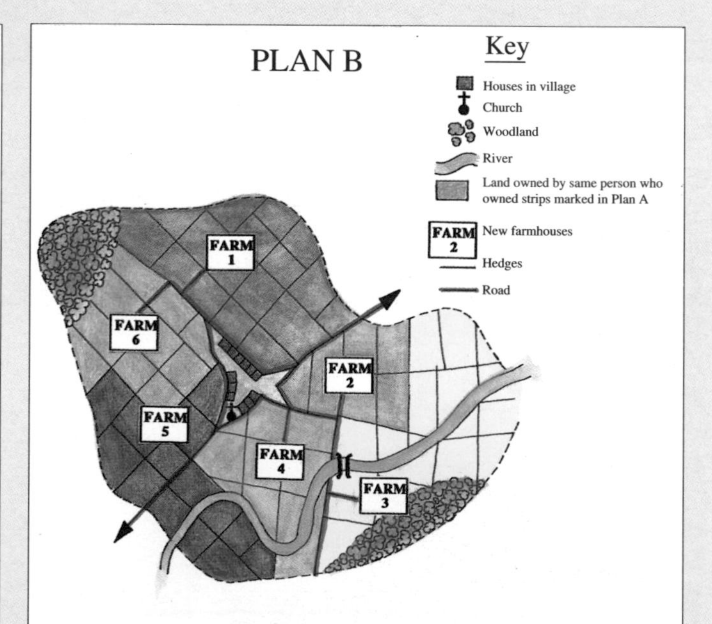

The same village after enclosure. The farmer who owned the strips marked on plan A now owned farm 2 in plan B. The common was also enclosed. Farms in plan B were owned by farmers who could prove that they had owned strips (they needed a legal document). Farmers might rent out enclosed fields or employ villagers to help them. It was now easier for farmers to plant different crops and to use new farming methods.

Source C Covent Garden in London in the late 18th century

The growth of population led to a demand for greater agricultural production. People living in towns could not grow their own food. The population of London grew from about half a million in 1700 to over 1 million in 1800. As a result, food markets such as Covent Garden grew rapidly.

Source D

I conversed with several farmers. One of them said that enclosing would ruin England. It was worse than ten wars. When I asked him what he had lost by it, he replied, 'I kept four cows before enclosure. Now I don't keep so much as a goose. And you ask me what I lose by it!' All declared that they could see no advantage in enclosures.

Arthur Young, 'Board of Agriculture Report on Bedfordshire', 1808

Source E

The open field farmers had been very poor and against enclosure but are now converted. The value of sheep's wool has gone up and the price of mutton has more than doubled. There are fewer cows but the land now produces more corn and is worth more. The poor are better employed. On the whole, the measure has been beneficial.

Arthur Young, 'General View of the Agriculture of the County of Lincoln', 1813

Activities

1. a) Use the figures in Source A to make a bar chart of enclosures between 1760 and 1830.

   b) In what years were the number of Acts greatest?

   c) Would you describe this process as 'rapid' or 'gradual'? Explain your answer.

2. Look at Sources B, D and E. Suppose you were the farmer whose strips are marked on plan A. What advantages did you have after enclosure? Why might other farmers have found enclosure to be a disadvantage?

3. Look at Source C. Suggest reasons why the growth of markets like Covent Garden may be linked to the spread of enclosure.

Changes to the land

For many years before 1700 some farmers had tried to improve the yield from their land by treating the soil and growing different crops. By 1771, Arthur Young (an agricultural writer) could talk of 'great improvements' in farming.

Spreading marl (a mixture of clay and lime) on sandy soil helps it to retain more water and makes it more fertile. Marling in Norfolk resulted in an increase in the value of land.

New crops began to be sown, especially in East Anglia. These were 'fodder crops' which provided food for animals and helped to restore nitrogen (an essential plant food) to the soil. When the animals grazed on land sown with these crops their manure also increased the fertility of the soil. A fallow year was no longer necessary. Crops could be grown every year. As a result, agricultural productivity increased.

Source A Greater specialisation

Source B New 'four crop' rotation

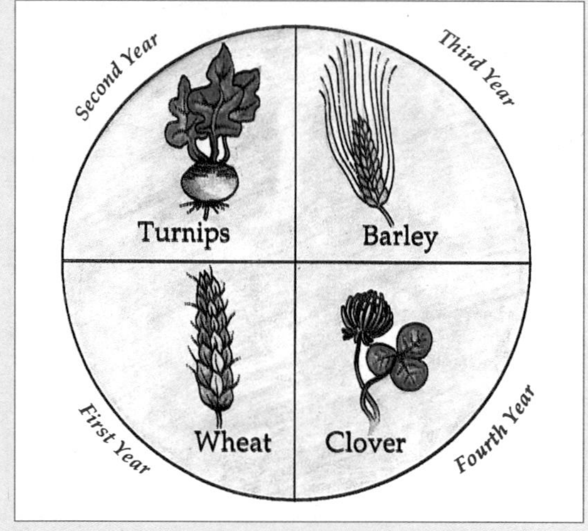

By growing fodder crops there was no longer a need for a fallow year.

Source C Improvements in farming

Great improvements have been made by the following means. FIRST, by enclosing land. SECOND, by spirited use of marl and clay. THIRD, by introducing an excellent rotation of crops. FOURTH, by the culture (growing) of turnips. FIFTH, by the culture of clover and rye-grass. SIXTH, by landlords granting long leases. SEVENTH, by the country being mainly divided into large farms.
Take any one from the seven and the improvement of Norfolk would never have happened.

Arthur Young, 'The Farmer's Tour Through the East of England', 1771

Activities

1. Study Sources A, B and C. Explain how the changes in farming would have increased productivity.
2. Many farmers were illiterate. They could not read about how to improve their land.

   Produce a poster to explain how one of the improvements mentioned on this page will help farmers to increase their productivity.

New animals

As more fodder crops became available animals did not have to be killed in the autumn. It was possible for an increasing number of farmers to feed large herds through the winter. Enclosure meant that animals no longer mixed together on the common. Hedges and fences provided shelter from bad weather. Disease was less likely to be passed from one animal to another. Interbreeding could be controlled. Some farmers specialised in breeding their animals scientifically to produce bigger specimens which would reach their full weight and maturity far earlier.

Source A Robert Bakewell's farm

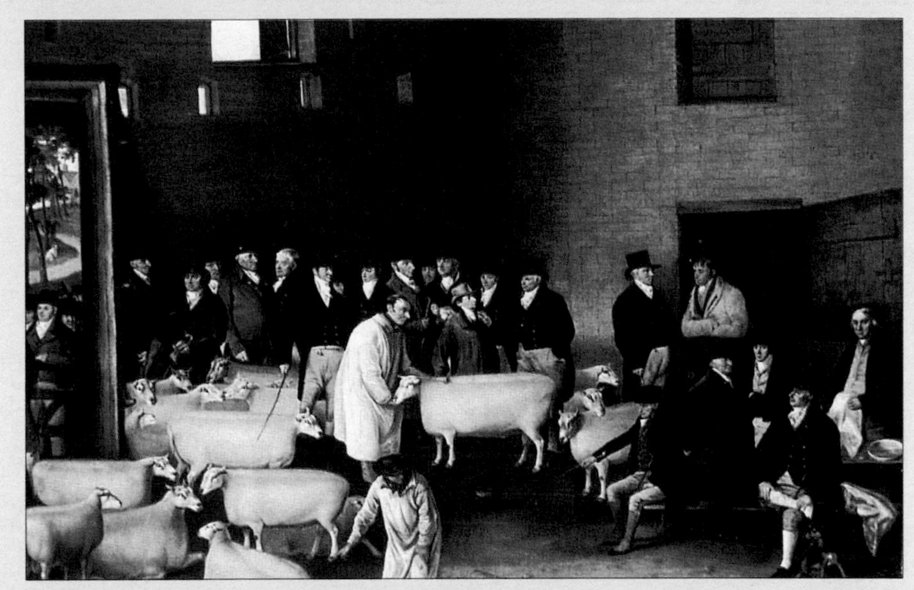

Robert Bakewell and other landowners tried to spread the word about selective breeding, new crops and new methods. In this picture Bakewell's rams are being hired out to mate with ewes at other farms.

Source B Bakewell's system

In tying up his cattle, Mr Toosey copies Bakewell's system. They are all tied up to straw or hay. They are fed with cabbages, littered well (cleaned out) and washed down twice a day. The sheep are equally well cared for. He gets 30s (shillings) to £3 for two-year-olds from the butchers.

Arthur Young, 'Tours in England and Wales', 1784

Source C

Selective breeding produced huge new animals like these prize pigs.

Source D Animals sold at Smithfield Market, London

	Average Weight in 1710	Average Weight in 1795
Cattle	370lb	800lb
Calves	50lb	143lb
Sheep	28lb	80lb
Lambs	18lb	50lb

Activities

It is 1790. You are a journalist who has been asked to write an article on the improvements in animal breeding in the 18th century. Include in your article interviews you might have had with: Robert Bakewell; Mr Toosey; a pig breeder and a butcher from Smithfield Market.

A golden age?

Between 1846 and 1875 farming boomed. 'High' farming (farming which aimed at maximum efficiency and profit) brought about many more changes in the countryside. New fertilisers became available. New breeds of animals were developed. The results of research were published to help farmers modernise their farms. Most notable was the increasing use of labour saving machines.

But changes often bring costs as well as benefits. A steam tractor operated by one or two people was able to do work which had previously required ten people. This meant that the landowner did not have to pay eight or nine people's wages and could produce more. But it also meant that those eight or nine workers could no longer rely on steady employment.

Source A Farming as a business

The best landlords in the country are said to be capitalists [owners of businesses] from the towns who, having purchased estates, manage them with the same attention to principles and details as gained them success in business. They drain their land thoroughly, remove useless timber, build suitable buildings and then rent to good tenants on fair terms. The rents are high but farms provided with every facility can far better afford to pay good rent.

James Caird, 'English Agriculture', 1850-51

Source B

The steam traction engine with 3 double ploughs ploughed about 8 acres in one day of 10 hours, at a cost for labour and coals of £1 12s, whilst the work performed by 6 single ploughs with 18 horses in the same time would only be 4 acres, and this at a cost of about £2 11s. The cost of buying the engine with the ploughs would be about the same as buying the 18 horses.

'Illustrated London News', August 1857

Source C Agricultural machinery at the Great Exhibition, 1851

By 1851 Britain had become the 'workshop of the world'. In that year, the Great Exhibition was held in London. The aim was to celebrate the progress being made in science, the arts and technology. A whole room in this exhibition was devoted to agricultural machinery.

Source D

This painting is called 'Hard Times'. As the use of machinery increased, there were fewer jobs available and farmworkers who did not own their own land had to travel to find work.

Source E Agricultural employment

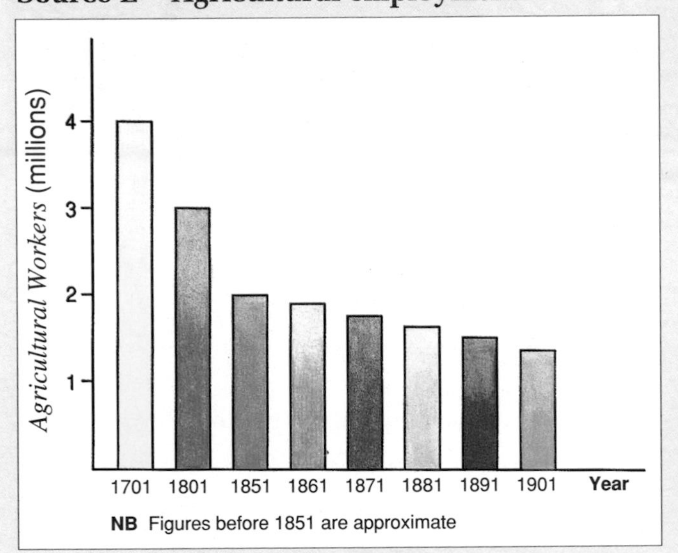

Source F Cartoon from 1863

Checklist

- Between 1750 and 1900 the British countryside changed dramatically. Strip farming in open fields was replaced by enclosed farms.
- New crops, methods and machines made farming more efficient and productive.
- As farms became larger and more mechanised, the number of farm workers fell.

Activities

1. Look at the sources on these pages.
   a) List the advantages and disadvantages of the changes in agriculture in the late 19th century.
   b) What evidence is there to suggest that change does not necessarily mean progress?
2. You have been asked to organise your own Great Exhibition to show the changes in farming between 1750 and 1900. What exhibits would you include? How would you make sure that you presented a balanced view?

3 INDUSTRY AND TRANSPORT

Before the industrial revolution industry was based in small workshops or in the home. Most goods were produced using hand-powered tools rather than machines.

Themes

Imagine a world without machines: no engines, electricity or gas; no planes, motor cars or trains; no factories. It would be very difficult to mass produce goods or to transport anything heavy or bulky.

In 1750 there was little mass production - the production of large quantities of the same articles by the use of machines. Despite this Britain was an advanced country compared to others. Banks provided finance for businesses. Shares in companies were bought and sold. There was a thriving export trade.

By 1900 Britain had become an industrial nation. New methods of production and new forms of transport had led to great change. Many historians describe the changes that took place as a revolution in industry and transport.

This chapter looks at the following questions.

- Why was there a revolution in industry and transport? What changes took place?
- What part did new technology play in the growth of industry and transport?

Focus Activities

1. Using the information on the Focus page draw a plan of Coalbrookdale as it might have been laid out. Mark on all the features mentioned by Arthur Young.
2. Why do you think Coalbrookdale was a good place to build an ironworks?
3. Do you think Arthur Young liked what he saw at Coalbrookdale? Give reasons for your answer.
4. 'In the late 18th century Britain was changing. It was becoming an industrial nation.' What evidence is there in the Focus to support this statement?

A visit to Mr Darby's ironworks at Coalbrookdale

In 1776 Arthur Young went on a tour of Shropshire. During his tour he visited the ironworks at Coalbrookdale. Until the 18th century iron was made by heating iron ore in a furnace fuelled by charcoal. Charcoal is made from wood. Coal could not be used as a fuel because chemicals from coal made the iron brittle - it broke easily. The ironworks at Coalbrookdale became famous because in 1709 Abraham Darby I (the first) discovered that coke rather than charcoal could be used to make iron. Coke is coal baked in a special way to get rid of the chemicals. In the passage below, Arthur Young describes Coalbrookdale as he found it in 1776. By then, Abraham Darby I was long dead and the ironworks were run by his grandson, Abraham Darby III.

Coalbrookdale by night

As I crossed the river by ferry I saw the place where Mr Darby says he will build his iron bridge. This bridge will be built of a single arch of cast iron stretching 120 feet across the river. I walked from the ferry and saw that the waggon ways which lead down to the river are laid with cast iron rails rather than wood. As full waggons are lowered down the rails they pull up the empty waggons from below. Then I saw the new mills. They are not finished yet but the immense wheels (20 feet in diameter and made of cast iron) are already in place and appear wonderful. I viewed the furnaces and forges with the vast bellows which give those roaring blasts. It makes the whole works horribly majestic.

These ironworks are thought to be the greatest in England. The whole process takes place here - from digging the iron ore to making it into cannons, pipes, cylinders and so on. All the iron ore used is mined in the neighbouring hills, as is the coal. The coal is made into coke, an invention of the greatest importance because the amount of wood in the kingdom has declined. Mr Darby employs nearly 1,000 people. The coal mines are from 60 to 120 feet deep.

Coalbrookdale itself is a very romantic spot. It is a winding valley between two immense hills thickly covered in wood. Indeed it is too beautiful to be suitable for that variety of horrors that industry has spread at the bottom of the valley. The noise of the forges, mills and so on with all their vast machinery, the flames bursting from the furnaces with the burning of coke and the smoke of the lime kilns are altogether dreadful.

Arthur Young, 'A Tour of Shropshire', 1776

Mechanisation

In 1750 Britain was not an industrial nation. By 1900 it was. What happened and why? Perhaps the most important development was the massive increase in mechanisation – the use of machines to produce goods. Inventions of new machines and new methods of powering them encouraged the growth of industry and different ways of working. The discovery of steam power was very important. In 1698 Thomas Savery invented a steam pump for draining mines. Before that time machines were powered by hand or by water. Improvements were made to Savery's steam pump during the 18th century. By 1781 James Watt had designed a steam engine which was far more powerful than water wheels. Mass production on a wide scale was now possible. By 1881 there were over 110,000 steam engines in Britain.

Source A James Nasmyth's steam hammer (invented 1839)

Steam engines provided greater power and control than was possible before. The 'Northampton Herald' said on 18 April 1846: 'the force of the blow which the steam hammer gives out is tremendous indeed. But it is under such control as to be made to drive a nail into soft wood with a succession of the most delicate taps.' The steam hammer was used to shape huge metal girders and bars required by industries such as shipbuilding.

Source B The impact of steam power

Mining

1. Steam engines needed coal for fuel, so more coal had to be produced.
2. Steam engines were used as pumps in coal mines, so deeper mines were possible.

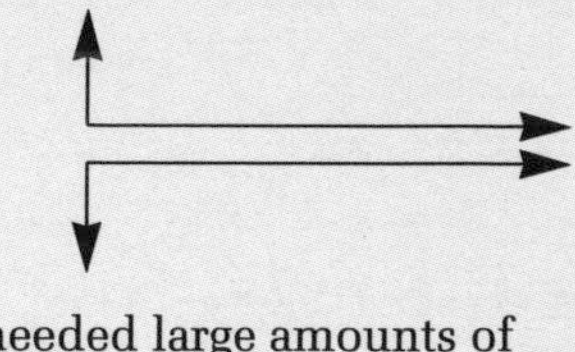

Transport

1. Steam engines needed large amounts of fuel (coal). This fuel had to be transported to the place where the engine was housed.
2. Steam engines drove locomotives which transported the fuel.

A steam engine

Factories

1. Steam engines and spare parts were built in factories.
2. Steam engines drove machines which made mass production possible. These engines were expensive and large and were therefore housed in factories.

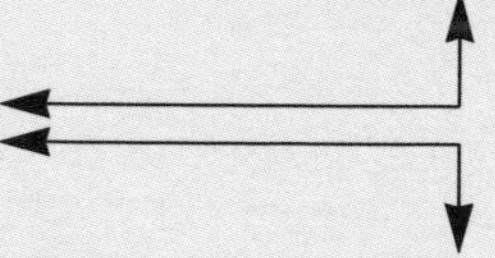

Iron

1. Steam engines were made of iron, so more iron had to be produced.
2. Steam engines drove machines which were used in the iron industry, such as the steam hammer.

Source C Inventions in the cotton industry

Date	Description
1733	John Kay Flying Shuttle for hand loom Hand power. Speeded up weaving Increased demand for thread.
1764	James Hargreaves Spinning Jenny Hand power. Increased supply of thin, weak thread.
1769	Richard Arkwright Water frame Water & then steam power Increased supply of strong, thick thread.
1779	Samuel Crompton Spinning mule Water & then steam power Increased supply of high quality strong, fine thread.
1787	Edmund Cartwright Power loom Water & then steam power Speeded up weaving Weavers able to use all that spinners could produce.

Source D Cotton production

Number of hours to spin 100lb of cotton

Date	Hours	Date	Hours
1700	50,000	1790	1,000
1780	2,000	1825	135

Value of cloth made

Date	£ millions	Date	£ millions
1770	12	1850	57.1
1821	49.6	1860	72.6
1836	53.4	1870	84.5

Growth of steam driven power looms

Date	Looms	Date	Looms
1785	0	1835	105,000
1813	2,400	1845	225,000
1820	14,000	1850	250,000
1829	55,500	1861	400,000

Source E

At the beginning of the current century, machines were simple and rarely seen. Agriculture could boast of nothing like machinery. Spinning and weaving were done by hand. Our ships were wafted by the breeze. Now all this has changed and there is scarcely a single manual operation which is not performed by mechanical aids. It is to the steam engine that the modern world owes its astonishing advances.

'Chambers' Journal', 10 October 1846

Source F

Who does not consider the use of machinery as one of the greatest evils there ever was in this country? Who would not rejoice at a return to the simple ways of work which allowed people to be healthy, happy and contented? Unless a great and speedy change is made in the laws about the use of machinery, we would advise people to declare war on it.

'The Union Pilot and Cooperative Intelligencer', 17 March 1832

Activities

1. Look at Sources A and B.
   a) List the advantages of the use of steam power.
   b) How did the use of steam power encourage the growth of industry?
   c) Design a poster advertising the steam hammer.
2. Look at Sources C and D. What effect did the invention of new machines have on the cotton industry? Explain how you know.
3. Look at Sources E and F. Describe what each author thought about the growing use of machines. How can both attitudes be explained?
4. You are able to visit Britain in 1700 and again in 1850. Using the sources on these pages note down the changes that have taken place and what you think of them.

Organisation, finance and growth of production

Suppose you worked out how to make a new machine. No matter how brilliant your invention was, it would only be of use (to anyone other than yourself) if you were able to build it and persuade other people to use it.

The growth of industry required money - capital. This was provided by capitalists - rich people who were prepared to invest in (put money into) projects. Inventors like James Watt relied on financial backing. Without the finance provided by Matthew Boulton, Watt would not have been able to build, perfect and sell his steam engine. The growth of industry also required reorganisation of the workplace. Many of the new machines were too large to put in a small workshop. Instead they were housed in purpose-built factories or 'mills' as they were often called.

Source A Arkwright's mill at Cromford in Derbyshire

The new machines invented in the 18th century were large and expensive. It made sense to house them in a special building (a factory) and to employ workers to come and work there. Although the first factory in Britain was built in 1717, it was only after Richard Arkwright built a number of successful factories in the 1770s that the idea began to spread. Arkwright's first factory at Cromford used water power. In 1780 he opened the first steam powered factory. Arkwright made a fortune from his business and has been described as the 'father of the factory system'.

Source B

I was excited by two motives to offer you my help which were love of you and love of a money-getting ingenious project. I presumed that your engine would require money. My idea was to set up a factory near to my own by the side of our canal. There I would set up all the things needed for the completion of engines. From this factory we would serve all the world with engines of all sizes.

Letter from Matthew Boulton to James Watt, 1769

Source C

I can on no account have anything to do with workmen, cash or accounts. I am not a man of regularity in business and have bad health. I would rather face a loaded cannon than settle an account or make a bargain.

Letter from James Watt to Matthew Boulton, 1769

Source D Growth of factories in Manchester

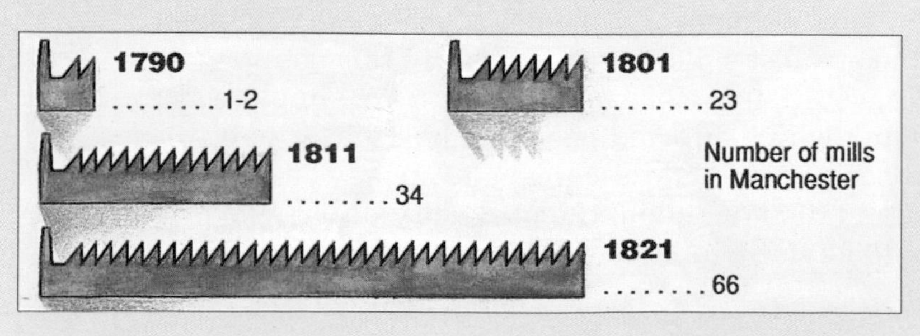

Source E Main centres and growth of industry in the 19th century

COAL PRODUCTION	
Year	Output (million tons)
1750	5
1800	11
1850	50
1900	225

IRON PRODUCTION	
Year	Output (thousand tons)
1750	30
1800	250
1850	2000
1900	9000

STEEL PRODUCTION*	
Year	Output (thousand tons)
1870	300
1880	1250
1890	3500
1900	5000

** Steel production was only possible on a large scale after the invention of the 'Bessemer converter' in 1856 and the discovery of the 'open hearth' process in 1866.*

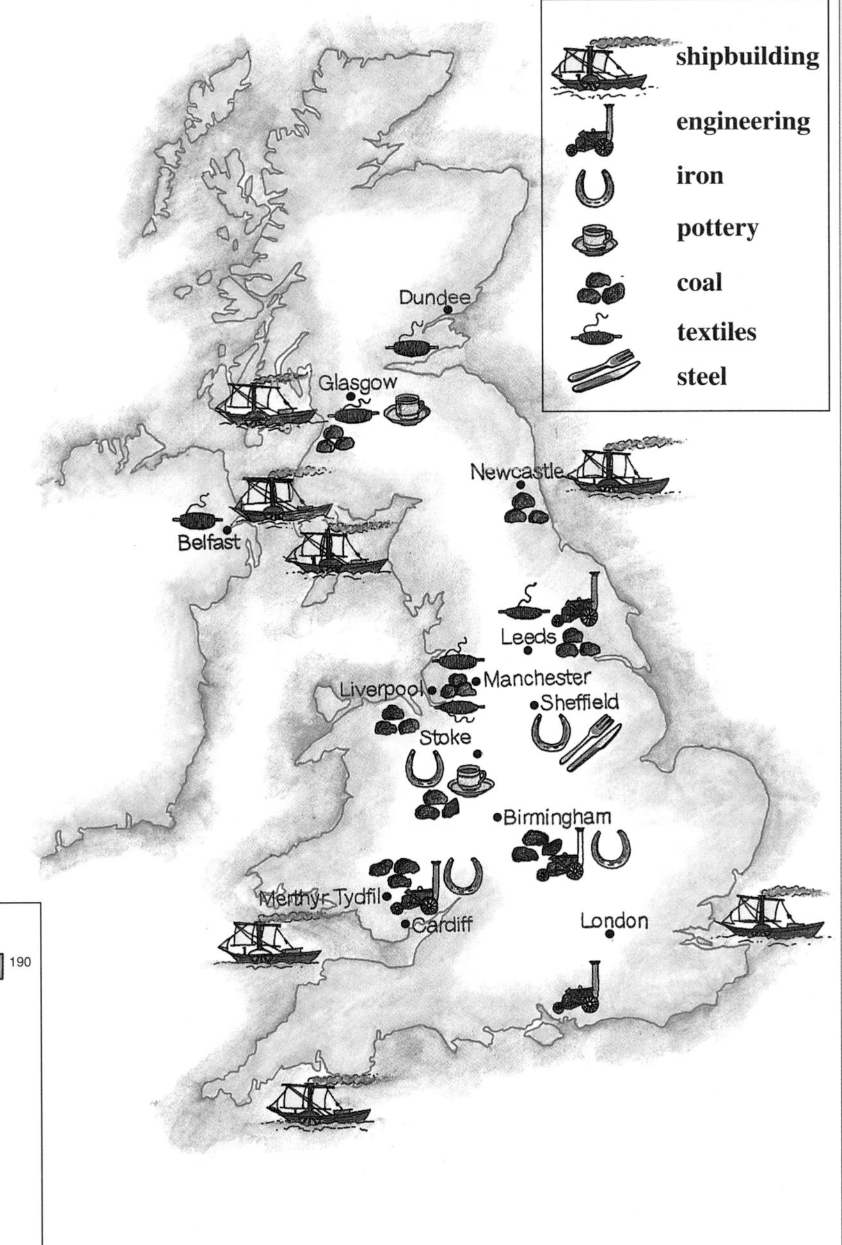

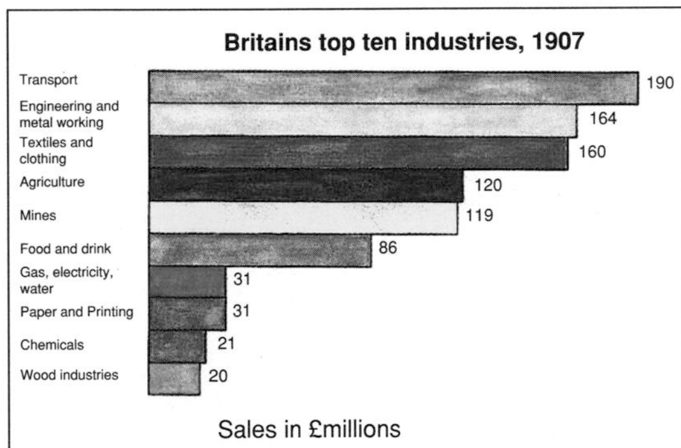

Activities

1. a) Look at Sources A, B and C. What advantages were there in setting up a factory rather than a small workshop?

   b) At first, factories used water power. What difference would the use of steam power make to the locations of new factories?

2. Use the sources on these pages to explain how finance and changes in organisation led to the growth of production between 1750 and 1900.

3. In the mid 19th century Britain was known as the 'Workshop of the World'. What evidence is there in Source E to suggest that this was an accurate description?

Changes in transport

In 1750 the quickest way to travel over land from London to Edinburgh was by coach. It took 11 days. Today it takes just 4.5 hours by train and less than 2 hours by plane.

In 1750 goods were transported by road, river or sea. This was not only slow, it was expensive. Between 1750 and 1900, however, roads were improved, a network of canals was built and the whole country gained access to the new railways. Transport did not just become quicker and more comfortable, it became cheaper and more efficient.

These changes in transport went hand in hand with changes in industry. Factories needed raw materials to drive their engines and to fuel their machines. These raw materials had to be transported to the factories and the manufactured goods taken to market. Equally, new forms of transport grew out of the changes in industry. The invention of the steam engine led to the development of steam locomotives and steam ships. These were made of iron and needed coal to drive their engines. Railways needed iron for their rails.

Changes in transport led to greater demand for steam engines, coal and iron. This greater demand meant more raw material had to be transported.

Source A Transport in 1837 and 1897

In 1897 this picture appeared on the front cover of the 'Illustrated London News'. It celebrated the changes in transport that had occurred during the 60 years of Queen Victoria's reign. The panels on the left show transport in 1837. The panels on the right show transport 60 years later.

Source B Cost of transporting one ton of goods, 1777

Route	By road	By water
Liverpool to Stoke	£2 10s 0d	13s 6d
Liverpool to Birmingham	£5 0s 0d	£1 5s 0d
Manchester to Leicester	£6 0s 0d	£1 10s 0d

Source C 'Past and Present Through Victorian Eyes', 1850

Source D

An industrial nation needs a cheap and safe way of transporting goods. This was the argument used for the introduction of canals and it is upon the same principle that railroads are now proposed. Railroads are a superior form of transport to those which now exist. Not only is transport by rail cheaper than by canal, it is also speedier.

Prospectus of the Liverpool and Manchester Railroad Company, 1824

Source E The three competing forms of transport, c.1840

The first canal was built in Britain in 1757. Canals remained an important form of transport until railways became established in the 1840s.

Activities

1. Look at Sources A, C and E. What does each picture tell us about changes in transport?
2. Look at Sources B, D, E and F. What advantages did canals bring? Why was the 'age of the canal' short-lived?
3. Using the sources on these pages explain how changes in transport and the growth of industry are linked.

Source F The canals at Birmingham

From here you may now go by canal to Hull, Liverpool, Bristol, Oxford and London. Coal before these canals were made cost 6d per hundredweight. It is now $4\frac{1}{2}$d. Every day during the six summer months 40 boats each carry 20 tons of coal.

Arthur Young, 'Annals of Agriculture', 1791

The business of transport

Improvement of the transport system was an expensive business. Imagine how much money you would need to pay for the construction of a new canal or a new railway. Although some people were rich enough to build their own transport system, usually a company was set up and shares were offered for sale. The money paid for the shares was used to build the canal or railway and each shareholder received a percentage of any profit made. In 1830 the first passenger railway line was opened. Once people realised that railways would be profitable they rushed to buy shares in new companies.

By 1847, over 600 companies had been set up. Some planned their railways carefully but many did not. A number of companies went bust and many investors lost their money. This rush to buy shares in railways is known as 'railway mania'.

Source A Josiah Wedgwood

Some canals were financed in the same way that Matthew Boulton financed the steam engine (see page 18). For example, in 1766 Josiah Wedgwood paid most of the money needed to build the Trent-Mersey canal. He did this so it would cost less to transport pottery from his factories in Stoke on Trent to the port of Liverpool (the price fell from £2 15s per ton to 15s per ton). A canal was especially suitable for Wedgwood's business since pottery is so fragile. In 1769 he built a new factory on the banks of the canal.

Source B Railway mania, 1844-47

This cartoon was drawn at the time of the 'railway mania'. It shows John Bull (the average Englishman) drunk with the thought of how much money he might make by buying shares in the new railway companies.

Source C Growth of railways

Cost of new railway lines	
Date	**Cost**
1844	£ 20 million
1845	£ 59 million
1846	£133 million

Length of track and profit		
Date	**Km of track**	**Profit (£ millions)**
1833	335	-
1843	3,225	6
1853	11,263	19
1863	17,055	30
1873	22,526	55
1883	26,065	68
1893	28,480	77
1903	30,892	107

Source D

What a revolution in business when the ordinary rate of travelling shall be 20 miles instead of 10 miles per hour! The traveller will live double time. By completing a distance in 5 hours which used to require 10, he will have the other 5 at his disposal. The man of business in Manchester will breakfast at home, proceed to Liverpool by the railway, transact his business and return to Manchester for dinner.

H. Booth, 1830

Source E

The railways transport goods at much lower rates. Coal, for instance, is carried at an average of ½d per ton per mile, while the canals charged 1½d. With all their faults, these iron roads have promoted the wealth of the people of this country. They save the public two thirds of their time and two thirds in fares. They have reduced the cost of many articles.

'Chambers' Journal', 1856

Source F Paddington station in 1862

Railway construction did not just involve building trains and laying lines. Stations were built and maintained and many people were employed as drivers, porters and ticket sellers. Railways were big business.

Activities

1. a) Look at Source A. Would you say that Wedgwood made a wise investment? Explain your answer.
   b) What other sources would be useful in order to provide a more informed answer?
2. Look at Source B. What was the artist trying to say about 'railway mania'? Explain how you know.
3. 'Most people gained from new forms of transport but some lost out.' Explain this statement using Sources A, B, D and E.
4. Using the sources on these pages design and write a brochure encouraging people to invest in a new canal or railway. Explain in the brochure why you need the money, what you would spend it on and why people should invest.

Checklist

- Between 1750 and 1900 Britain became an industrial nation.
- Increased mechanisation, the growth of factories and the willingness to invest in new ideas all played a part in the growth of industry.
- Advances in industry were matched and helped by improvements in transport.
- Like industry, changes in transport required new technology and finance.

4 POPULATION AND TOWNS

A modern 'dream' kitchen

Welwyn Garden City – a new town planned and built after the First World War

Themes

Today more than 55 million people live in the United Kingdom. In 1750 the total population was about 7.5 million. It is difficult to be exact because no census – population count – took place until 1801. After 1801 a census was held every 10 years. The census figures between 1801 and 1901 show that there was a rapid growth in population.

In 1750, there was only one town with a population of over 100,000 – London. By 1851, ten towns had a population of over 100,000 and over 2 million people lived in London. In 1750 about 20% of the population lived in towns but by 1851 this figure had risen to 55%. By 1901 70% of the population lived in towns.

The rapid growth of population and of towns is linked to the changes in agriculture and the growth of industry. More people needed food, clothing, houses and jobs. Towns expanded as industry grew. This brought a new way of life and new problems.

This chapter looks at these questions.

- How and why did towns grow?
- What was it like to live in the new industrial towns?
- What improvements were made to town life during the period 1750-1900?

Focus Activities

1. Judging from the interview on the Focus page would you say that Chadwick's report had been accurate? Explain your answer.
2. Suppose that you had lived in Whitechapel in 1843. Write a description of your home and its surroundings explaining why there is a high death rate in the area.
3. What recommendations do you think the Commission should make? Design and write the report.

Life and death in Whitechapel

In 1842, Edwin Chadwick (a lawyer concerned about living conditions in towns) published a report which claimed that many towns contained areas where people lived in squalor (poor, filthy conditions). The following year, the government set up a Royal Commission to find out whether Chadwick's report was accurate. The Commission's job was to conduct interviews and, if necessary, to suggest improvements. The following is just one of many interviews.

Interviewer Mr Liddle, how would you describe the living conditions of poor people in Whitechapel?

Liddle (a doctor) Truly appalling.

Interviewer And the water supply?

Liddle Water is laid on to very few houses. Most people get their water from a hole in the courtyard. When I have visited their rooms, they have very little water in their tubs. When they are washing, the smell of dirt mixed with soap is disgusting. The filth in their houses is dreadful, so is their personal filth. When they come to my surgery, I always have to keep the door open.

Interviewer And how do they get rid of their dirty water?

Liddle There is not one house with a sink. There is also a shortage of sewers. Sewage lies around the place in a most offensive condition.

Interviewer Would you say that these public nuisances are one cause of the high death rate and, if so, what happens to the corpse when someone dies?

Liddle Yes, they are a cause of death. The problem is that nearly all families have only one room. The corpse is therefore kept in the room where people sleep and have their meals. Bodies are kept for a full week, sometimes longer.

Interviewer What do the family do?

Liddle What I see when I first visit is that people do not seem to notice. The family is found eating or getting on with their usual business.

Interviewer I must say, I find this shocking. Thank you Mr Liddle...*(Liddle exits)*...I suppose we'd better start on our report. How shall we begin?

The growth of towns

Between 1750 and 1900 the birth rate was higher than the death rate. In other words there were more births than deaths. This meant that the population went up.

The increase in population was one of the factors that led to the growth of towns – especially industrial towns. Once steam power had been developed factories could be built almost anywhere. These new factories needed workers who needed houses. So towns grew up around the factories. The goods that were produced had to be moved to market and so ports and other trading centres had more business and people moved to them too.

People moving to towns also created jobs. Houses had to be built and inns and shops opened. But there was no control and no planning. Landlords built new houses where and how they liked. These houses were built quickly and cheaply and were packed together. Often they lacked basic facilities like running water. As a result the new towns brought new problems.

Source A Population of Britain

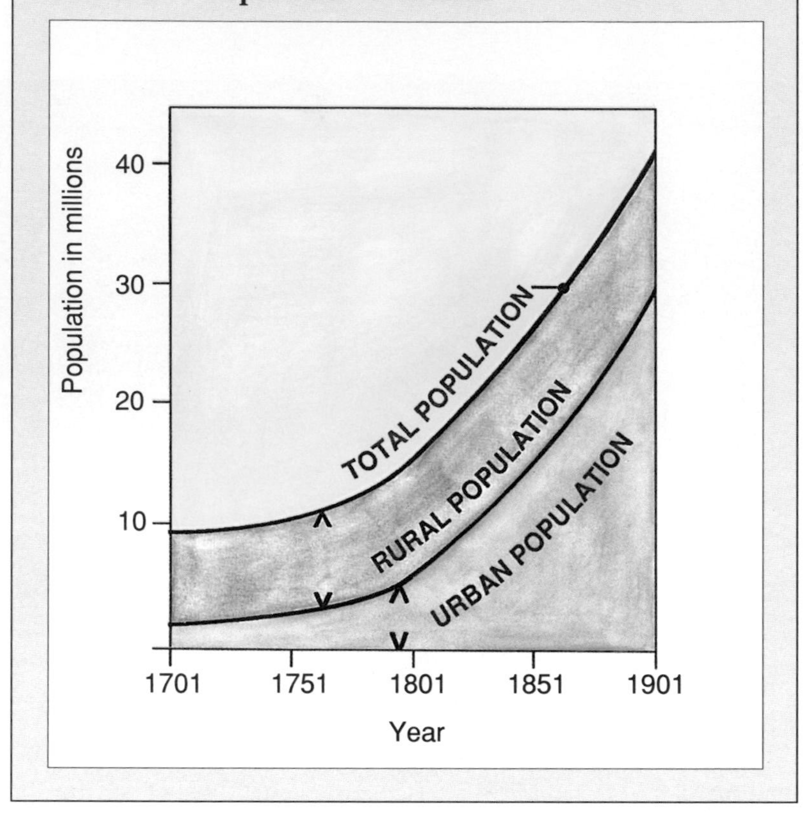

Source B Population of towns (in 1,000s)

Town	1750	1801	1851	1901
London	100	1,172	2,685	6,586
Liverpool	35	82	376	685
Manchester	45	75	303	645
Birmingham	30	71	233	522
Leeds	14	53	172	429

Source C The growth of Birmingham

About 50 years ago there were only three principal streets in Birmingham. Today it is a crowded and extensive town. This illustrates, in a very striking manner, the rapid increase of our industry and trade in steel and iron.

W. Thompson, 1788

Source D

New houses are built with astonishing rapidity. They have no foundations. The walls are only a half-brick thick and the materials are unfit for the purpose. A man who had built a row of these houses visited them one morning after a storm and found them all levelled to the ground. They are built back-to-back without ventilation or drainage. Double rows have perhaps a water pump at one end and a privy (toilet) at the other. These are used by about 20 houses.

Mr Mott's evidence to the House of Lords, 1842

Source E

Each landlord builds as he pleases. New houses, with or without cellars, huddled together row behind row may be seen springing up in many parts. These rows may be badly drained, the streets may be full of stagnant water but no one may find fault. Manchester has no public park where the population can walk and breathe fresh air. New streets are extending in every direction.

Report of the Committee on the Health of Towns, 1840

Source F Sheffield in the 1730s and 1850s

Activities

1. Look at Source A and explain what this graph tells us about the changing population in Britain.
2. What do Sources B and C tell us about the growth of towns?
3. Look at Sources C, D, E and F. Would you describe the growth of towns as progress? Explain your answer.
4. Look at Source F. Suppose you had been able to visit Sheffield in the 1730s and again in the 1850s. Describe the changes that would have made the biggest impression on you.

Living in towns

What was it like to live in these new towns? The answer depends on which group of people you look at.

For rich families, life could be very comfortable. Many lived in beautiful, large houses. Servants looked after them and their diet was full and varied.

It was a different world for the poor. Poor areas quickly became dirty, smelly and overcrowded slums. Life in them was a constant struggle for survival. No wonder rich people built their houses in the areas where the prevailing wind did not blow towards them.

Source A **A rich family at home**

Source B

My vacation has been spent visiting the worst parts of the worst towns with Mr Smith and Dr Playfair. Dr Playfair has been seriously ill. Mr Smith has had a little dysentery. Sir Henry de la Beche was obliged at Bristol to stand up at the end of an alley and vomit while Dr Playfair was investigating overflowing toilets.

Edwin Chadwick, 1843

Source C **A poor family at home**

Source D

In the first house I turned into there was a single room. The window was very small and the light came in through the door. The young woman said, 'Look there at that great hole; the landlord will not mend it. Every night I have to sit and watch, or my husband does, because that hole is over a common sewer and the rats come up twenty at a time. If we did not watch for them they would eat the baby up.'

Lord Shaftesbury, 'Description of Frying Pan Alley', 1847

Source E The diets of two families interviewed by S. Rowntree in 1899

FAMILY 1	Breakfast	Dinner	Tea	Supper
Monday	Porridge, fried bacon, toast, butter, treacle, marmalade, tea, coffee.	Boiled mutton, carrots, turnips, potatoes, caper sauce, roly-poly pudding, rice pudding.	Bread, teacake, butter, cake, tea.	Fish, bread, butter, cake, biscuits, cocoa, oranges.
Tuesday	Porridge, fried bacon and eggs, toast, butter, marmalade, coffee, tea.	Mutton, carrots, turnips, caper sauce, potatoes, tapioca pudding.	Bread, cereals, butter, marmalade, tea.	Cutlets, stewed plums, bread, biscuits, cheese, cocoa.
Wednesday	Cereals, fried eggs, bacon, toast, butter, marmalade, coffee, tea.	Rissoles, poached eggs, potatoes, bread pudding.	Bread, butter, teacake, cereals, tea.	Baked haddock, stewed plums, biscuits, hot milk.
FAMILY 2				
Monday	Bacon, bread, tea.	Bacon, bread, tea.	Bacon, bread, tea.	None.
Tuesday	Bread, meat, tea.	Meat, bread, tea.	Meat, bread, tea.	None.
Wednesday	Bread, bacon, tea.	Meat, bread, tea.	Eggs, 'dip', bread, tea.	None.

Source F A family in Liverpool 1911

Five of these children lived in a four bedroomed terraced house. Their father worked in newspaper production. All became healthy adults. The other five lived next door in a two bedroomed house. Their father worked in a factory making lead paint. Four of them died young of tuberculosis (a lung disease).

Source G

If there's anything extra to buy, such as a pair of boots for one of the children, me and the children go without dinner - or maybe only 'as a cuppa tea and a bit of bread, but Jack 'ollers (shouts) to take his dinner to work and I give it 'im as usual. He never knows we go without and I never tells 'im.

Interview in 'Poverty: A Study of Town Life', by S. Rowntree, 1901

Activities

1. Suppose that you were invited to spend a week in the home shown in Source A and then a week in the home shown in Source C. Using the other sources, describe your experiences and feelings about the homes.
2. A 19th century writer claimed that the lives led by the rich and the poor were so different that Queen Victoria ruled over two nations - a poor nation and a rich one. What evidence is there on these pages to support this idea?
3. What reasons can you suggest to explain why one of the families in Source F remained healthy and the other did not?
4. Use the information on these pages to write a report for the government on health and housing, 1830-1900.

Better living conditions

Today we complain about the litter in our towns and the exhaust fumes from cars but we do not expect to see piles of rubbish and sewage in the streets or floating in our rivers. We take it for granted that our council will see that rubbish is collected and that the Water Authorities will provide sewers to take away our waste. We expect to live in houses with running water and flush toilets.

But 150 years ago, people could not take these things for granted. Many people rejected the idea of laws about public health and housing. It was only after cholera epidemics and a long campaign that the problems caused by the rapid growth of towns were tackled.

Source A Cholera

In 1831 an outbreak of cholera killed over 30,000 townspeople. The cause was unknown but people thought it was linked to dirty conditions. Despite demands for action it was not until a second outbreak in 1848 that a Public Health Act was passed allowing town councils to make improvements. Opposition continued because improvements were costly but, from 1848, better sanitation and growing medical knowledge helped to stamp out cholera and other diseases such as typhus and dysentery.

Source B London, 1849

Let the streets of London be called by their proper names. That is to say, let them be called by the various nuisances or diseases that overrun or pollute them. Let them be called 'Open Sewer Street', 'Slaughter House Buildings', 'Knacker's Yard', 'Grave Yard Crescent' or 'Typhus Terrace'. At least let that be their name until this filthy capital has been properly drained and watered, until its atmosphere has been disinfected and until plague and disease have been stamped out.

We understand that several farmers have applied to the London Water Companies for a supply of liquid manure. The water supplied by these companies is said to contain all the right ingredients.

'Punch', 1849

Source C Town councils

In 1875 town councils became responsible for public health by law. Improvements, such as slum clearance and new sewers, were paid for by the rates, a local tax.

Liverpool Council sees that the citizen's house is properly built and sometimes even builds it. It brings an unfailing supply of pure water. It sweeps the streets and disposes of rubbish. It provides travel to work. It gives the citizen books to read, pictures to look at and music to listen to.

R. Muir, 1907

Source D Life expectancy

In 1750 a person's life expectancy was approximately 36 years (it is difficult to be exact since no records were kept). This table shows how life expectancy has changed since figures have been available.

Date	Male	Female	Date	Male	Female
1851	39.9	41.8	1951	66.5	71.5
1901	44.1	47.8	1991	72.4	78.1

Source E   Technological advance

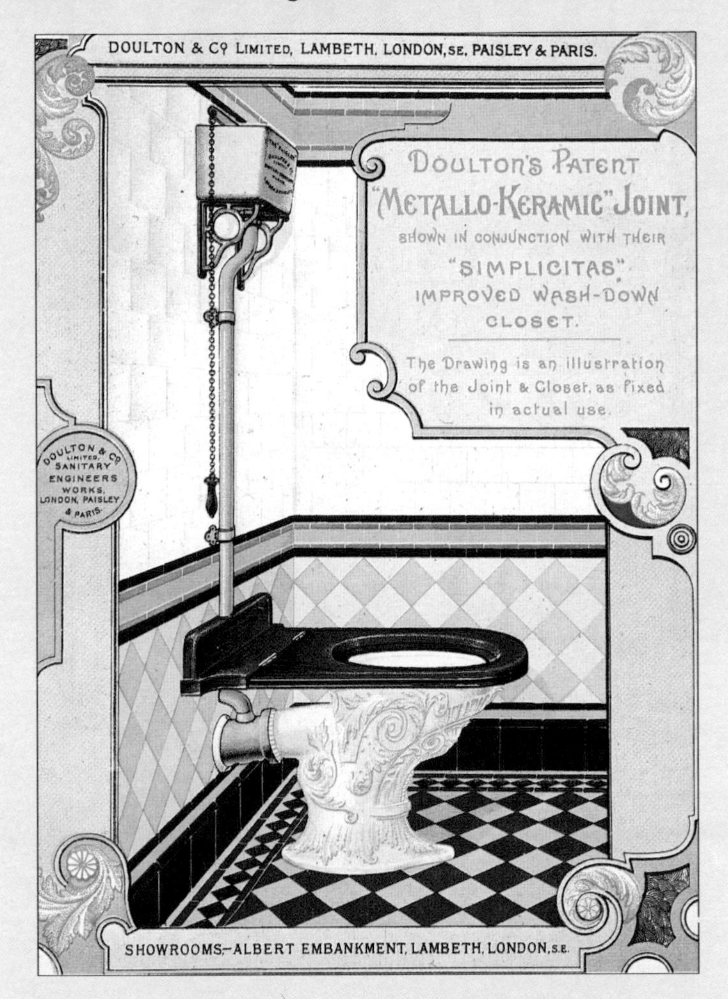

The flush toilet was invented in the 18th century but was too expensive for most people. In 1870 Twyfords invented a cheaper version but it was not until this century that most people could afford a flush toilet.

Checklist

- Between 1750 and 1900 the population of Britain rose dramatically.
- Many people moved into towns. By 1851 more people lived in towns than in the countryside.
- The rapid growth of towns was unplanned. There was poor housing and bad sanitation. Many people lived in squalid conditions.
- Improvement only came slowly and many problems were still unsolved by 1900.

Source F   Life in the 1980s

Andrew Tsokallis is a roofer. He and his wife have 2 children. They live in a council flat on the 11th floor of a tower block in Hackney, London. The flat is tiny and cramped. Ants and cockroaches get in through the hot-air ducts. Bernadette describes their life:

'For food, I'll go and buy us a pound of chops or 10 beefburgers for £1. That does us for a couple of days. Nothing for sandwiches. Andrew goes out in the morning without breakfast and he can't afford no dinner. Sometimes he complains that his belly hurts him. I cry sometimes that I can't afford clothes for the kids. Everything we've got is what's been given them or second hand. We've never been out since we got married. We're just stuck in here every night watching telly.'

Paul Harrison, 'Inside the Inner City', 1985

Activities

1. What do Sources A and B tell us about living conditions in towns in the 19th century?
2. You are a town councillor in 1875. Use Source C to design and write a leaflet proposing ways to improve your local town.
3. Source E shows one technological improvement. Make a list of other improvements to life in towns.
4. What evidence is there on these pages to show that between 1851 and today:
   a) living conditions have improved
   b) living conditions have not improved?
5. Suppose that Source F described your family. How would that affect your answers to Question 4?

5 EMPIRE AND TRADE

The Queen and Commonwealth leaders

On Christmas day every year the Queen's broadcast to the British Commonwealth (a community of nations which have ties with Britain) is watched by millions of people all over the world. The countries of the British Commonwealth have many different religions, races, languages and governments. But they all share in the same history. They were all at one time a part of the British Empire.

In 1750 the British Empire was expanding. A number of colonies (areas abroad under British rule) had been set up. Between 1750 and 1875 the Empire grew slowly but during the next 25 years lands nearly 40 times the size of Britain were added to the Empire. By the beginning of the 20th century Britain ruled over 13 million square miles of territory and about 370 million people.

This chapter looks at these questions.

- How and why did the Empire grow?
- What were the relations between British people who went to the colonies and the people who lived there already?
- What impact did the Empire have on Britain?

The Falklands war, 1982

British forces were sent to the Falkland Islands in the South Atlantic after Argentina invaded them. The islands became a British colony in 1833.

Focus Activities

1. Suppose you were a British journalist in South Africa in 1879. You reach Isandhlwana on January 30th. Write an article for a British newspaper which explains what had happened.
2. How would you expect the British public to react to the news?
3. Write an account of the battle from the point of view of the Zulus.

The Battle of Isandhlwana, 22 January 1879

In 1879 the British army fought a war against the Zulus in South Africa. The Zulus were armed mainly with spears and clubs whilst the British had guns and swords. Although the Zulus won the battle of Isandhlwana, they suffered between 2,000 and 3,000 casualties. The British lost 800 soldiers and 500 of their African troops – there were hardly any survivors. Despite this defeat the British army won the war against the Zulus later that year. Below, a British survivor and two Zulu warriors describe what happened at Isandhlwana.

A painting of the Battle of Isandhlwana

Eyewitness account of Lieutenant Horace Smith-Dorrien, one of the few British survivors of the battle

The Zulus were seen coming over the hills. They were in the most perfect order. Nobody knows how many there were but the general idea is at least 20,000. Before we knew it they came right into the camp. Everyone who had a horse turned to fly. The place where their line seemed thinnest was where we all made for. We ran over ground covered with huge boulders and rocks until we got to a deep gully. As I passed a poor fellow of the mounted infantry who was wounded in the arm, he asked me to bandage his wound. I used my handkerchief to stop the bleeding. As I did so, Major Smith came past, wounded, and said, 'For God's sake get on, man. The Zulus are on top of us'. I turned to jump on my horse but it was hit by a spear and leapt into the gully. I gave up all hope. The Zulus were all around me finishing off the wounded – the man I helped and Major Smith among them. I rushed off on foot and plunged into the river. I was being carried downstream at a tremendous pace when a loose horse came by me. I grabbed its tail and it landed me safely on the other bank. I got up and rushed on. A few Zulus followed me for about three miles across the river but they had no guns. I had a revolver and I kept letting them know it. They finally stopped altogether.

Eyewitness account of two Zulu warriors

1. When we closed in we came to a mixed group of mounted and infantry men. They numbered about 100. They made a desperate resistance, some firing with pistols and others using swords. But we were too many for them and killed them all where they stood.

2. It was wonderful. Every warrior shouted 'coward' as he killed one of them.

Growth of Empire

Until the 1870s the main reason for building an Empire was to protect trade. From the 1870s, however, a new word began to be used - 'imperialism'. Imperialists wanted a bigger Empire not just to increase trade but also to increase Britain's power in the world. They also believed that 'uncivilised' parts of the world needed to be 'civilised'. By this time other European countries were also building their own Empires. There was a race to grab control of the lands of Central and Eastern Africa (which had recently been explored by Europeans for the first time). This is known as the 'Scramble for Africa'.

Source A David Livingstone

The first step towards the expansion of the Empire was the exploration of new lands. This picture shows the explorer David Livingstone shortly before his death in Africa in 1874 (like many Europeans in Africa he suffered from malaria). On a visit to Britain in 1857 Livingstone said, 'I go back to Africa to open a path for commerce and Christianity'.

Source B

I was in the East End of London yesterday and attended a meeting of the unemployed. I listened to the wild speeches which were just a cry of 'Bread! Bread!'. On my way home I thought about this and became more convinced of the importance of the Empire. In order to save the 40 million inhabitants of Britain from a bloody civil war, we colonial statesmen must gain new lands to settle the surplus population and to provide new markets for the goods produced by factories and mines. The Empire, as I have always said, is a bread and butter question. If you want to avoid civil war, you must become imperialists.

Cecil Rhodes, businessman, Prime Minister of Cape Colony and first British ruler of the African country known as Rhodesia (now Zimbabwe), 1895

Source C

When an Englishman wants a thing he never tells himself he wants it. Instead, he waits until the idea comes into his head that it is his moral and religious duty to conquer those who have the thing he wants. Believing that he is a great champion of freedom, he conquers half the world and calls it 'colonisation'. When he wants a market for goods from Manchester, he sends a missionary to teach the natives the Gospel. The natives kill the missionary. The Englishman then flies to arms in defence of Christianity, fights for it, conquers for it and takes the new market as if it were a reward from heaven.

George Bernard Shaw, 'The Man of Destiny', 1898

Source D

It is said that our Empire is already large enough and does not need extension. That would be true enough if the world were elastic, but it is not. At present we are 'pegging out claims for the future'. We have to remember that it is part of our heritage to take care that (as far as it can be) the world is shaped by us. It must receive an English-speaking character and not that of other nations. We have to look forward to the future of our race. We should fail in our duty if we decline to take our share of the division of the world.

Lord Rosebery, speech made in 1893

Source E The growth of the British Empire in the 19th century

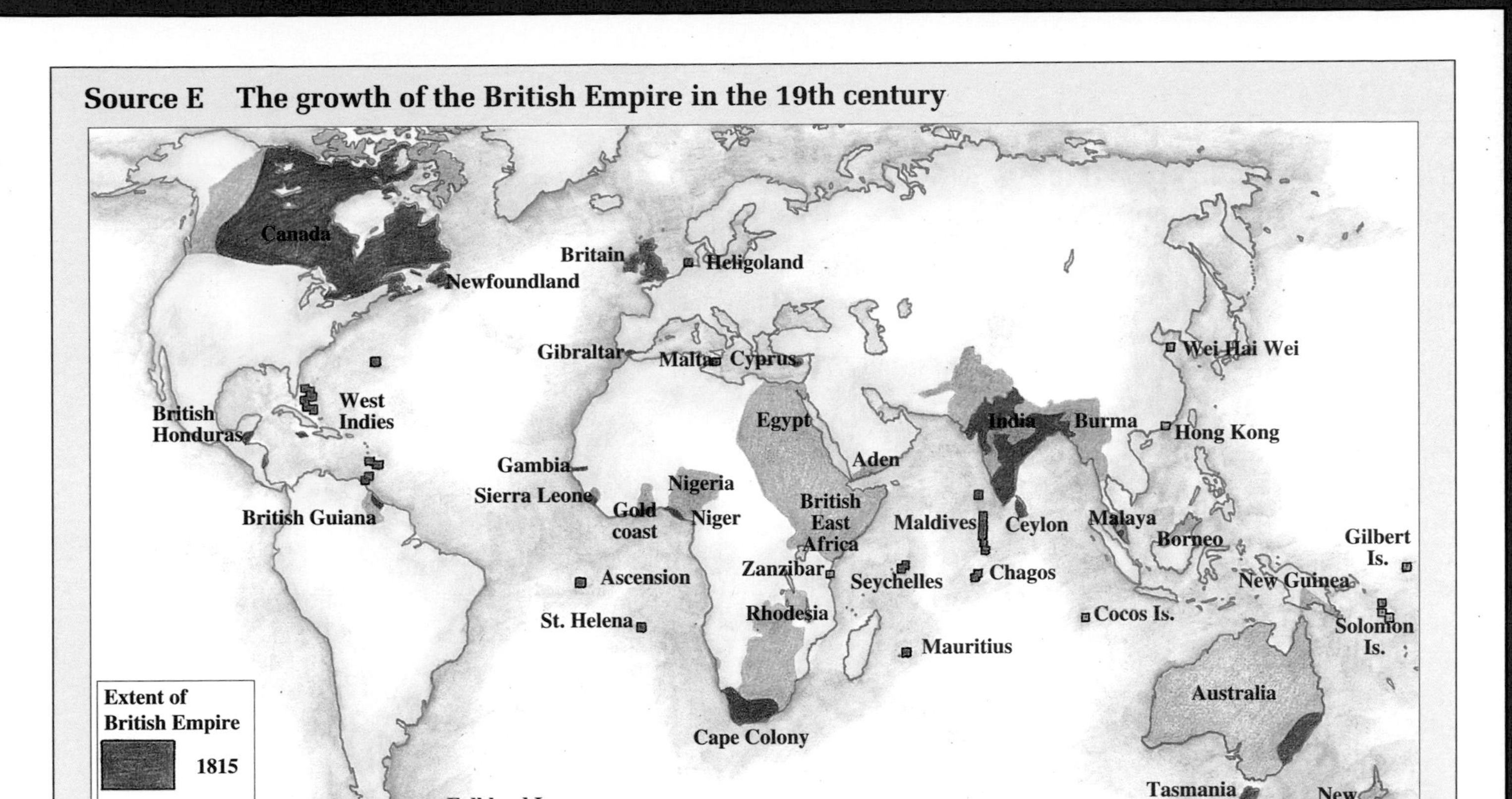

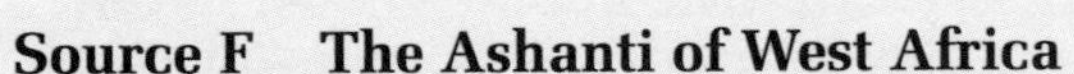

Source F The Ashanti of West Africa

British officers being entertained by the King of the Ashanti. The British were often welcomed by local rulers and treated as special guests.

Activities

1. Look at Source A.
   a) What part did explorers like Livingstone play in the growth of the Empire?
   b) What does this Source tell us about Livingstone's attitude towards Africans?
2. a) Using Sources B, C and D explain why British people wanted the Empire to expand. List your reasons under these headings: *political, religious, economic* and *other*.
   b) How does the attitude of the author of Source C differ from the authors of Sources B and D? Explain your answer.
3. 'By 1900 Britain ruled the waves.' How does Source E show that this was the case?
4. Look at Source F. Do you think that the Ashanti were wise to welcome the British like this? Use Sources B, C and D to support your answer.

Trade

The growth of industry and the growth of the Empire are linked together by the need for foreign trade. Sea-power made Britain a trading nation well before 1750. Raw materials (such as cotton from India) were brought to Britain, made into a finished product (such as cloth) and then sold abroad. The success of this trade encouraged the growth of industry. As industry grew, more goods were produced and there was therefore a need for greater foreign trade (more raw materials were needed and there were more finished goods to sell). The colonies of the British Empire played an important part in this trade cycle. They provided a steady supply of raw materials to Britain where they were converted into a finished product. This finished product was often then sold back to people who lived in the colonies.

Source A Imports and exports 1700-1900 (£ million)

Year	Imports	Exports
1700-09	4.8	6.1
1740-49	7.3	9.9
1800-09	28.7	37.6
1840-49	79.4	141.5
1900-09	570.4	333.3

Source B

The silk of China is woven in Coventry and sold wholesale in New York. It is then shipped to New Orleans where it is sold to a planter. That American planter grows cotton which is exported and woven into cloth in Manchester. This cloth is sold in Bengal in India by a trader. The trader may be paid for it partly in produce (tea/spices). This produce is sold in the English market 10,000 miles away.

W. Felkin, 'The Exhibition of 1851'

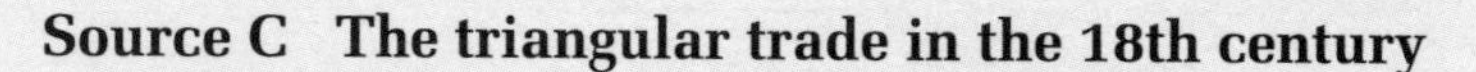

Source C The triangular trade in the 18th century

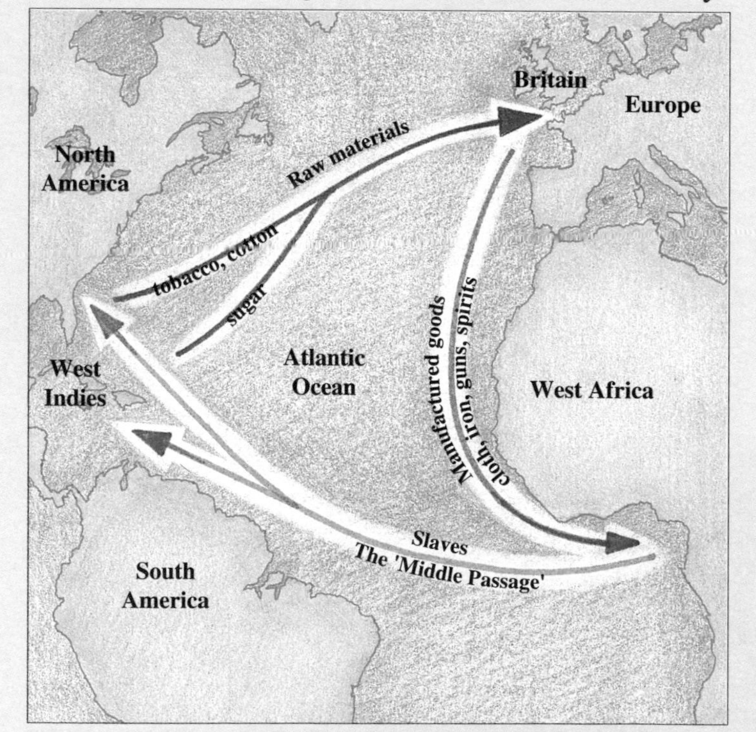

Ships sailed from Britain with manufactured goods which were exchanged for slaves in West Africa. The slaves were shipped across the Atlantic and sold to plantation owners in North and South America and the West Indies. The ships then returned to Britain loaded with the products of the plantations. Britain abolished the slave trade in 1807.

Source D
Britain's industrial output compared with that of other countries 1780-1900

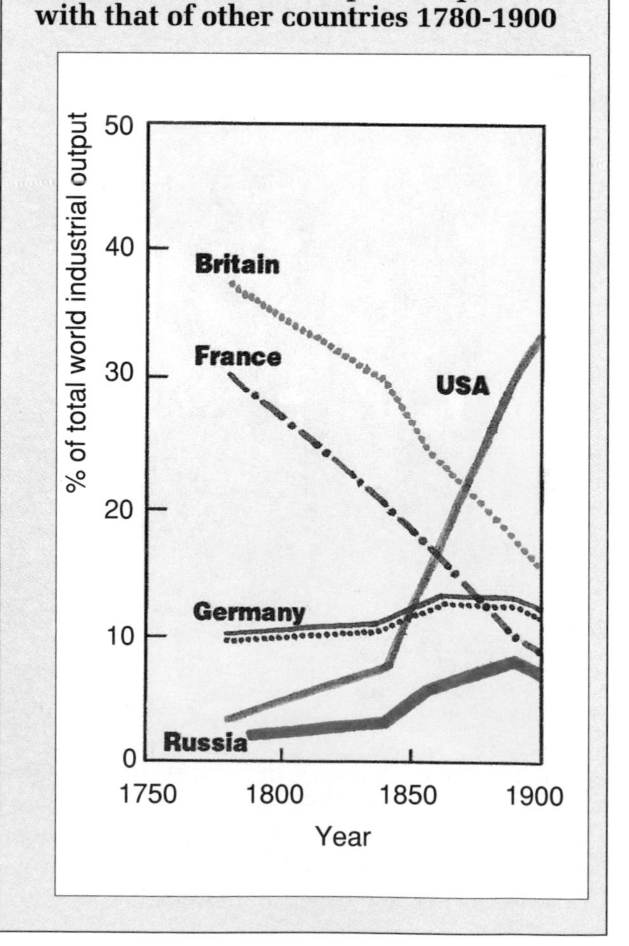

Source E Britain's trade routes in 1900

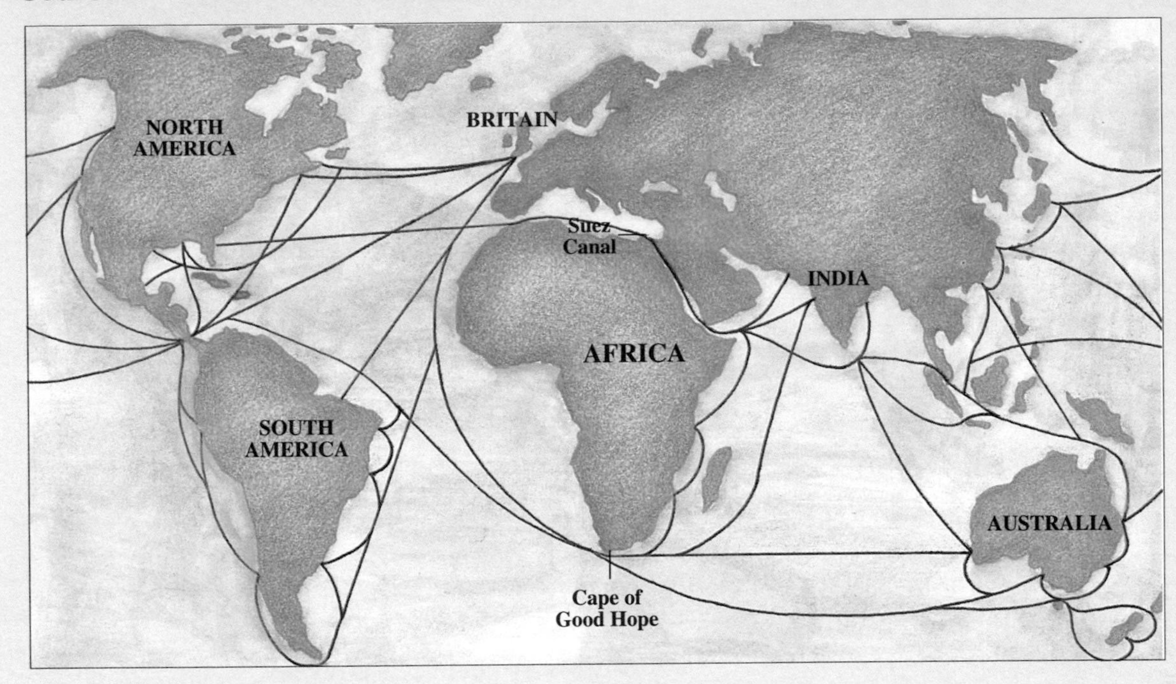

Until 1869 traders travelled between Britain and India via the Cape of Good Hope. In 1869, however, the Suez Canal was opened. This allowed traders to make a much quicker and safer voyage.

Source F

In 1875, the Egyptian leader, the Khedive, decided to sell his 44% of the shares in the Suez Canal. The British Prime Minister, Disraeli, immediately arranged to borrow £4 million from the bankers Rothschild's and beat the French in the race to buy the shares. As a result Britain was able to safeguard trade with India. Disraeli told Queen Victoria:

It is just settled. You have it, Madam. Four million pounds! There was only one firm that could do it - Rothschild's. They behaved admirably; advanced the money at a low rate; and the entire interest of the Khedive is now yours, Madam.

Benjamin Disraeli, 1875

Source G

We have spoken already of the vital necessity of new markets. It is therefore to our obvious advantage to teach the millions of Africa what it means to be civilised. Then we can supply goods to them in return for the products of their country and the labour of their hands. We want the African clothed because our looms will clothe him. We want him housed and furnished because our Sheffield firms will supply what is needed. We want his fields to double their produce and that produce to be of high quality because it is needed by our manufacturers in England.

Lord Lugard, 'The Dual Mandate', 1922

Activities

1. What do Sources A and D tell us:
   a) about the development of British trade between 1750 and 1900?
   b) about the development of world trade?
2. What do Sources B, C and E tell us about the patterns of trade which developed in the 18th and 19th century? Draw a diagram to illustrate Source B.
3. Using Sources E and F explain why Disraeli wanted to buy shares in the Suez Canal.
4. Look at Sources D and G. How did competition from other countries affect Britain's attitude towards trade within the Empire at the end of the 19th century?

'Civilising' the world

According to Queen Victoria the aim of the British Empire was to 'protect the poor natives and to advance civilisation.' There was clearly more to the growth of Empire than just trade. British imperialists believed that they were superior to the native peoples of the colonies, especially if those people were black. Even when slavery was abolished most white people in Britain continued to think that they were naturally superior to black people. This affected the way in which the colonies were ruled.

Source A

I will lay down my policy on this native question. Either you will receive the natives (black people who lived in South Africa before colonisation) on an equal footing as citizens or call them a subject race. I have made up my mind. The native is to be treated as a child and denied the vote.

Speech made by Cecil Rhodes, Prime Minister of Cape Colony (South Africa), 1894

Source B

At heart every Briton considered as his inferior everyone who was not white - the less white, the more inferior.

James Morris, 'Heaven's Command', 1973

Source C

Sir Harry Johnston, a colonial administrator, realised how useful the missionary might be to Her Majesty's Empire. He said, 'Missionaries strengthen our hold over the country, they spread the use of English language, they teach the natives what it means to be civilised. In fact each mission station is a lesson in colonisation.'

J. Pettifer and R. Bradley, 'Missionaries', 1990

Source D African saying

When they first came they had the Bible and we had the land. We now have the Bible and they have our land.

Source E A Maori chief being baptised in New Zealand

In the New Testament a passage urges Christians to spread the message: 'Go ye therefore and teach all nations' (Matthew 28:19). When Britain began to gain an Empire it was considered both a duty and an opportunity to bring Christianity to the 'godless' people of the newly discovered lands. Christians who travel abroad to try and convert people to Christianity are called 'missionaries'. During the 19th century many missionaries travelled to the colonies. Missionaries often tried to convert the chief of a tribe first, knowing that the rest of the tribe would probably follow this lead.

Source F A new railway in India in the 1880s

A train has come off its tracks. British supervisors (dressed in white) take charge. The British brought new technology to the colonies.

Source G

Ceylon (now Sri Lanka) was unified under British rule in 1815. Over the next 80 years the British built 2,300 miles of road and 2,900 miles of railway. They raised the area of land used for farming from 400,000 acres to 3.2 million acres, the livestock from 230,000 to 1.5 million, the post offices from 4 to 250, the telegraph lines from 0 to 1,600 miles, the schools from 170 to 2,900, the hospitals from 0 to 65, the annual amount of goods shipped abroad from 75,000 tons to 7 million.

James Morris, 'Pax Britannica', 1968

Source H Australian poster, 1816

This poster aimed to show native Australians (Aboriginals) that British justice was fair. In fact, Aboriginals were often hunted and killed for sport in the 19th century.

Activities

1. Look at Sources A and B.
   a) What do these sources tell us about the attitudes of white British imperialists? Have attitudes changed since then?
   b) Do you think Cecil Rhodes' refusal to allow native people the vote was fair? Explain your answer.
2. Suppose you are a missionary in Africa. Using Sources C and E write a letter home explaining what you hope to do and how your mission will help the British to govern the colonies.
3. What does Source D tell us about the attitude of Africans to British rule?
4. Using Sources F and G, explain what advantages British rule brought to the native peoples of the colonies. Why might they not have seen them as advantages?
5. a) Why do you think the poster in Source H was produced? What is its message?
   b) What other sources would you wish to look at to build up a more reliable picture of relations between the British and Aboriginals?

Britons abroad

As the Empire grew so did the number of British people who left Britain to live in the colonies. Although the British government sent only a small number of officials to run each colony, many traders and settlers went to live there. The colonies were not just 'civilised' for the benefit of the native peoples. The Britons who moved to the colonies expected to benefit. They wanted a better standard of living than they had at home.

Source A

The British who lived in the colonies liked their creature comforts and were able to enjoy them more luxuriously than they generally could at home. With their hordes of servants and privileges, they could live in a class above themselves.

James Morris, 'Pax Britannica', 1968

Source B An Imperial Durbar

Although Queen Victoria was the Head of the Empire, she never left Europe. Her representatives in the colonies lived in splendid luxury and had complete control over affairs within their colony. This painting shows the Viceroy (British Governor) of India at an 'Imperial Durbar'. A durbar was a special ceremony. Princes and local leaders from all over India came to show their support for the Queen and her Viceroy.

Source C

Let us visit, for a taste of imperial club life at its most agreeable, the Hill Club at Nuwara Eliya in Ceylon (now Sri Lanka). This little town lay high among the tea estates. The British had laid out a park with a maze and a botanical garden. They had dammed a little lake. They had marked out gentle walks around the surrounding woods and named them after great ladies of the colony – 'Lady Horton's walk' and so on. There was a big half-timbered Grand Hotel and a cottage for the Governor of Ceylon with a pond and croquet lawn. There were the inevitable golf and race courses. There were villas strung about the lake, an English church, of course, and a lending library.

James Morris, 'Pax Britannica', 1968

Source D A life of luxury

Many people enjoyed life in the colonies because they could expect greater luxury than they had at home.

Source E   Convicts working in Tasmania, 1830

Some of the first settlers in Australasia (Tasmania is an island just south of Australia) were convicts whose punishment was to be 'transported' there. This began in 1788. The convicts were made to work on government projects such as road building or on the land owned by free settlers. After serving their sentence they often had the choice of returning to Britain or staying in Australia. Transportation as a punishment ended in 1867.

Source F   Emigration

Between 1800 and 1914 about 14 million people emigrated from England, Wales, Scotland and Ireland. Most went to the USA, Canada and Australasia.

Our readers will no doubt recall that a government grant was made to assist families and single men, being of good character, to emigrate to Australia. The number was limited to 5,000 and amongst these were included a portion of single women and girls between 18 and 30 years of age. Unhappily there exists in England so much real distress that anything in the shape of improving conditions must be good. It is true that the voyage is long and there is unpleasantness in a crowded ship. But where there is health and strength and a willingness to labour, they are soon forgotten.

'Illustrated London News', April 1844

Source G   Letter from Canada

Dear Father and Mother,

I like the country here very much. I got work the first day I was here and have had plenty of work ever since. Farmers and labourers all sit at one table here. I know that a poor man can do a great deal better here than he can at home. He is sure to get plenty of work if he is steady, and can live cheaper. We work here from sunrise to sunset but we do not work as hard as we do at home.

'Letters from Sussex Emigrants', edited by the Reverend T. Sockett, 1832

Activities

1. You are a rich British traveller in 1890. Use Sources A, B, C and D to describe the benefits of the British Empire.
2. What evidence is there in the pictures in Sources B and D to support the view expressed in Source A?
3. Use Source C to draw a plan of the Hill Club at Nuwara Eliya. Suppose you were a local who worked in the tea estates and watched the British using the club. Write a letter describing what you thought of British rule in Ceylon.
4. Look at Sources E, F and G. How did the growth of the Empire help the British government to cope with problems at home?

The colonised

When the British arrived in a new land the people they met there knew nothing of the English language or the British way of life. The British often took advantage of this and imposed British rule. Even though they claimed that their aim was to 'advance civilisation' they treated the native peoples as second class citizens. There were few serious rebellions against British government before 1900. But the experience of native peoples under British rule in the 19th century was a major cause of later discontent.

Source A **A slave being mistreated on board ship**

Slaves did not only suffer beatings on board ship. Conditions were so overcrowded and dirty that many died during the voyage.

Source B

Under ancient slavery slaves could obtain their freedom and even rise to the very top. But with colonial slavery a slave ceased to be regarded as a person at all. A slave had no legal rights and was treated as a thing to be bought and sold for profit. A slave was used in the same way that a factory owner would use a machine.

'Roots of Racism' published by the Institute of Race Relations, 1982

Source C

I hate the British for the wrong they have done in India. Their Parliament makes laws for us and their government appoints a Viceroy to rule over us. The British are arrogant, despising our brown skins. Worst of all, the British have kept us poor. Our people toil for slave wages in British-owned cotton mills and on British-owned tea plantations.

Pandit Nehru, India's first Prime Minister after India became independent in 1947

Source D **Signing the Treaty of Waitangi, New Zealand, 1840**

By signing this treaty Maori chiefs transferred ownership of their land to the British. White settlers then divided up the land and fenced it off. Before the British arrived Maoris had no idea that people could own land (it belonged to everyone) and they did not make written treaties. It is unlikely that the Maoris would have agreed to a treaty if they had fully understood what it meant.

Source E   Indian workers loading cotton bales onto ships, c.1880

Cotton was transported to Britain where it was made into cloth. The men dressed in white were in charge of the workers. Many workers in the colonies were paid very low wages.

Source F

Davarum was 30 years old when he put his thumbprint to a document he could not even read: 'We agree', it said, 'to serve the employer chosen by the Natal government under Act 14 of 1859 and we all understand the terms under which we are employed.' Davarum (or 'Coolie Number 1', as the recruiting officer named him) had no idea where Natal was nor did he understand Act 14. But he, like thousands of others, was prepared to travel anywhere to escape the poverty of India. On 12 October 1860 he, his wife (Coolie Number 2) and their two children (Coolie Number 3 and Coolie Number 4) joined 388 others aboard the *Truro*. A few hours later, the dangerously overloaded vessel began its long journey to South Africa.

'Illustrated History of South Africa: The Real Story', edited by Dougie Oakes, 1988

Source G

When Gandhi landed at Durban in South Africa in May 1893 he had recently qualified as a lawyer. He had to travel to Pretoria. First class accommodation was purchased for him and he boarded the train for an overnight journey. At Maritzburg, a white man entered the compartment, eyed the brown intruder, withdrew and then reappeared with two railway officials who told Gandhi to transfer to third class. Gandhi protested that he had a first class ticket. That didn't matter. He had to leave. He stayed. So they fetched a policeman who took him off. Gandhi could have returned to the train and travelled third class. But he chose to remain in the waiting room all night. Many years later in India, Dr J. Mott asked Gandhi, 'What have been the most creative experiences in your life?'. In reply, Gandhi told the story of the night in Maritzburg station.

'The Life of Mahatma Gandhi', Louis Fischer, 1951

Activities

1. What evidence is there in Source A to support the view expressed in Source B?
2. Look at Source C. What evidence is there in the other sources to support the criticisms made of the British?
3. Using Sources D and F explain how the British took advantage of people who did not fully understand them.
4. Look at Source G. Gandhi later became leader of a campaign to end British rule in India. Retell his story as he might later have told it. Include in your version an explanation of what this event taught him about British rule in the colonies.

What the Empire did for Britain

The 'Scramble for Africa' in the 1880s was a race between Britain and other European nations to gain control of as much land in Africa as possible. Unlike the expansion of the Empire earlier in the century, there was little concern with trading possibilities. The main aim was to gain power and prestige. Supporters of the Empire wanted other countries to look up to Britain and (just as important) they wanted the British public to be proud to belong to such a great Empire. There was opposition to this type of imperialism. In 1879 William Gladstone, a leading politician, said, 'In every corner of the globe British imperialism is causing pain.' But by the time of Queen Victoria's Diamond Jubilee in 1897 there was a mood of triumph in Britain.

Source A Spoils of Empire: Sezincote, a country house

This house was built in Gloucestershire in 1805. It was designed and paid for by Sir Charles Cockerell who, after making a fortune in India, retired to Britain. Not only was the house built in an Indian style, it was furnished with many articles brought back from India.

Source B Heroism: the Battle of Isandhlwana, 1879

A scene from the battle described on the Focus page. By the time this was painted it was well known that the British had lost this battle. The artist shows heroic British soldiers fighting to save their company's flag (which had been captured by the Zulus). This may never have happened in reality. Pictures like this aimed to make the British public proud of their Empire.

Source C

Before she set out on her Diamond Jubilee procession on the morning of 22 June 1897, Queen Victoria went to the telegraph room at Buckingham Palace. In a matter of seconds her Jubilee message was on its way to every corner of the Empire. The procession itself was a superb display. 50,000 troops marched in two columns to St Paul's for a thanksgiving service. British troops led with representatives from the colonies behind. Crowds lined the streets with welcoming banners and fluttering handkerchiefs. Cheers rolled across London. There was the thump of drums and the singing of patriotic songs. Thousands of Union Jacks flew from towers and from windows or waved in the hands of school children. Everybody agreed that it was a great success.

James Morris, 'Pax Britannica', 1968

Source D Queen Victoria's Diamond Jubilee, 1897. Indian troops march past.

People from all parts of the Empire were represented in the procession – for example there were Chinese policemen from Hong Kong, soldiers from Canada, Australia and South Africa, Indian Princes and people from Malaya, Nigeria, Jamaica and New Zealand. Never before had the British public seen such evidence of the size of the Empire and the variety of its people. The 'Daily Mail' claimed that there was not a person in the crowd who 'did not gain a new view of the glory of the British Empire'.

Checklist

- During the 18th and 19th centuries Britain's Empire expanded greatly. By 1900 Britain ruled the largest Empire the world had ever known.
- The British believed they had the right to rule the Empire. They wanted power, to protect their trade and to 'civilise' other people.
- Black people were regarded as inferior by the British. Even after the abolition of slavery black people in the colonies were treated as second class citizens.
- The Empire helped the government to solve problems at home. It encouraged people to be patriotic and gave people the opportunity to enjoy a better lifestyle in the colonies.

Activities

1. Look at Source A. Why do you think Sir Charles Cockerell built and furnished his house in this style? What do you suppose local people thought about it?
2. Suppose you had seen the picture in Source B at an exhibition in 1885. Describe your reaction to it and write a short story or poem based on it.
3. Look at Sources C and D.
   a) What information does Source C add to that provided by Source D? Where do you think the author of Source C obtained this extra information?
   b) Suppose you were a member of the crowd watching the procession. Describe what happened and what you thought about it.

6 WORKING CONDITIONS AND REFORM

Modern factories are very different from those in the 19th century. This factory is automated – much of the work is done by robots.

A boy weaving cotton in India. Child labour still continues in some parts of the world.

Today we take it for granted that young children should not be made to work for a living. We expect the owners of factories and businesses to make sure that the workplace is safe for their employees. We assume that people will only have to work for a limited number of hours each day. There are laws which control working conditions. But this was not always the case.

When Britain first became industrialised there were no laws controlling working conditions. Hours and pay were decided by the owners of factories and mines. They could treat their workers as they liked. Some treated them well but very many did not.

This chapter looks at the following questions.

- What was it like to work in factories and mines in the 19th century?
- How and why did working conditions change and what effects did the changes have?
- Why were trade unions set up and what did they do?

Focus Activities

Matthew Crabtree's answers in the Focus passage were typical of those given to the Sadler Committee. Suppose you had been a member of the Sadler Committee in 1832:

1. Write a report about Matthew Crabtree's working conditions showing why you find them unacceptable.
2. What other questions might you have asked the workers?
3. Make a list of changes which would make working conditions better.
4. Explain how you would make sure that factory owners made these changes.

The Sadler Committee

In 1832, a Parliamentary Committee interviewed a number of people who had worked in factories since they were children. The Committee's report was then presented to Parliament in the hope that a law banning child labour would be passed. The following is just one of many similar interviews.

Child labour in a cotton mill

Interviewer	Matthew Crabtree
What age are you?	Twenty two.
What is your job?	I make blankets.
Have you ever been employed in a factory?	Yes.
At what age did you first go to work?	Eight.
What were the normal hours of work?	From 6 in the morning to 8 at night.
How long were your breaks?	An hour at noon.
What were your hours in busy times?	From 5 in the morning to 9 at night.
How far did you live from the factory?	2 miles.
Was it easy for you to be punctual?	No. I rarely woke up on my own. My parents had to get me out of bed and dress me while I was still asleep.
What happened if you were late?	I was beaten.
Are workers often beaten?	Yes, all the time.
Why?	The machine worked at the same rate all day. Therefore the supervisor had to keep us working at the same rate too. We were beaten to stop us falling asleep or working slowly.
What did you do when you got home?	All that we did when we got home was to eat the little bit of supper that was provided for us and go to bed immediately. If supper had not been ready straightaway, we should have fallen asleep while it was being prepared.
Was it the same for the other children?	Yes, for all of them. But not all lived so far from work as I did.
Were you afraid of what might happen if you were late?	When I got up I was so scared of being beaten for being late that I used to run and cry all the way to the mill.

Working in factories

Building factories was expensive. Most factory owners were concerned with making a profit, not with spending money on providing good conditions for their workers. This meant that pay was usually low and hours long. People were expected to work in a dangerous or unhealthy environment. The machinery in many of the cotton mills in Lancashire, for example, was so loud that workers became deaf. There were no safety covers over moving parts of the machinery and accidents were common. But complaining often meant the sack. The population was growing and many people were looking for jobs.

Source A Factory Rules, 1844

1. Any weaver absent after the engine starts in the morning – 3d fine for every loom in their charge.
2. Weavers leaving the room without asking permission – 3d fine.
3. All broken brushes, wheels, windows etc – to be paid for by the worker.
4. Any worker seen talking, whistling or singing – 6d fine.

Many factories had rules like these. Workers might be fined for sneezing, swearing, reading, laughing, opening a window or leaving an oil can out of place.

Source B Women workers in a cycle factory in Coventry in the 1890s

The man on the left is the supervisor. None of the machines have safety guards.

Source C

A jam factory

The condensed steam drops down from the roof so that you are not surprised that the thin cotton dresses the girls wear are soaked and even their hair is dripping wet. In a resigned manner, they admit that 'it's a bit steamy'.

Marie Paterson, 1880

Source D Bleach powder packers

The packer has to enter a chamber which has been filled with chlorine gas. Though the worst of it has been allowed to escape, the atmosphere is still charged with deadly fumes. The heat is tremendous. Gassing is such a common matter that the men would describe it as they would tell you what their Sunday dinner was like.

Home Office Report, 1893

Activities

1. What do the sources on this page tell us about:
   a) working conditions in factories
   b) workers' attitudes towards these conditions?
2. How would you expect working conditions to differ today?

Working in mines

The demand for coal to power steam engines, iron smelting and railways resulted in miners going deeper and deeper underground in search of coal. This was very dangerous. Miners feared explosions of 'firedamp' (methane gas) set off by the candles they used for light; suffocation from 'chokedamp' (carbon dioxide); rockfalls; flooding and accidents on the way up and down the shaft. Lung diseases were very common and young bones became deformed from hours spent crouching in narrow tunnels.

Source A Mining today

A miner cutting coal in a modern mine

Source B

Young girls, married and aged women carried burdens of coal of up to 3 hundredweight on their backs, often through water up to their knees or from the bottom up ladders to the surface. They also did the hard work of cutting the coal with the men or dragged trucks on all fours harnessed by chains.

Gertrude Lewis, 'Recollections of my grandfather Dr Southwood Smith', 1898

Source C Conditions in mines in 1842

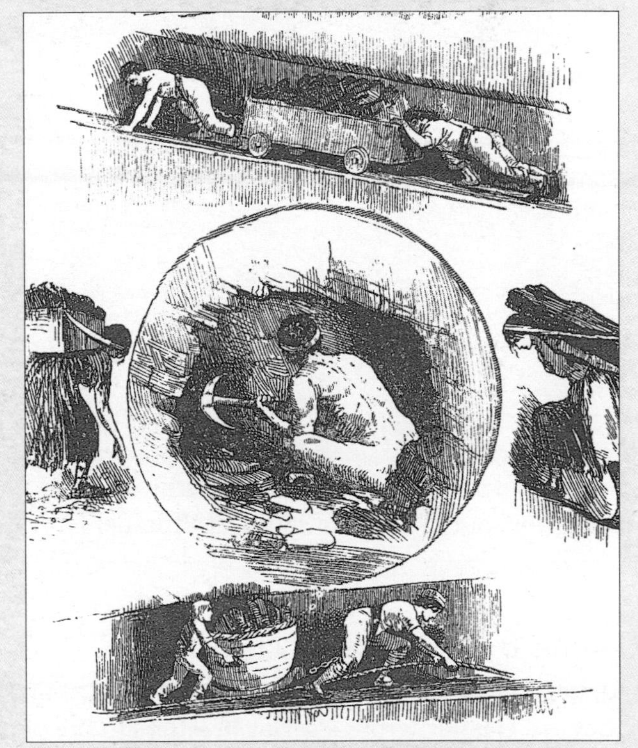

These pictures appeared in a report presented to Parliament in 1842. Most MPs had never been inside a mine and did not know what it was like to work in one.

Source D Mining memories

The thin seams of Durham were a nightmare. When you crawled down the seam, only inches would separate the roof from your body. Your head would be flat against the floor with maybe a two inch space above you before you hit the roof. You would 'swim' forward, arms straight out in front, legs behind, wriggling.

Dave Douglass, a miner in the 1870s

Activities

1. Using the information on this page, write the report to go with the pictures in Source C. What improvements in working conditions would you suggest?
2. Look at Source A. What changes have taken place since the mid 19th century? What has remained the same?

Arguments about reform

It was not just child labour in factories and mines that caused concern. Many people believed that a woman's place was in the home looking after her husband and children. By working she was seen to be depriving a man of a job. Reformers argued that the government should introduce laws banning child labour and limiting the hours worked by women. Opponents of reform, however, argued that new laws were unnecessary and would be harmful. The government was reluctant to act until large numbers of people began to demand changes.

Source A

Under the present law, no mill which employs persons under the age of 18 (and therefore scarcely any mill at all) can be worked more than 11 hours a day. In a mill so worked, the whole profit is made in the last hour. So, if the hours of working were reduced by one hour per day, profit would be destroyed.

N. W. Senior, 'Letters on the Factory Act', 1837

I have visited many factories. The children seemed to be always cheerful and alert. The work of these lively elves seemed to resemble a sport. Conscious of their skill, they were delighted to show it off to any stranger. As to exhaustion, they showed no sign of it. After work, they skipped around with the same energy as boys coming out of school.

Dr Andrew Ure, 'The Philosophy of Manufactures', 1835

Source B

Boys working in a cotton mill in Clitheroe, Lancashire

Source C

Illustration from 'The White Slaves of England' by John Cobden, 1860

Source D The slaves of England

Shocked by a visit to a Bradford woollen mill in 1830, Richard Oastler wrote a series of letters to the papers under the title 'Yorkshire Slavery'. He compared children's working conditions to slavery in the colonies.

Thousands of little children, both male and female, aged 7 to 14 years are forced daily to labour from 6 in the morning to 7 in the evening with only – Britons blush whilst you read it – with only 30 minutes allowed for eating and recreation.

R. Oastler, letter to the 'Leeds Mercury', 16th October 1830

Source E 'Dinner Hour at Wigan', 1878

The women worked in the cotton mill in the background.

Source F

A vast majority of the persons employed at night, and for long hours during the day are women. Their labour is cheaper and they put up with physical tiredness more easily than men.

Parliamentary Papers, 1843

Source G

When the woman goes out to work everything runs to waste. The house and children are deserted. The wife can do nothing for her husband and family. Dirt, discomfort and ignorance reigns. Females are forming clubs and meet together to drink, sing and smoke. They use the lowest, most brutal and most disgusting language imaginable. A man came into one of these clubrooms with a child in his arms. 'Come, lass', he said, 'come home for I cannot keep this child quiet and the other I have left crying at home.'

Speech made by Lord Shaftesbury, 1842

Activities

1. Using Sources A, D, F and G, list the arguments for and against:
   a) the employment of children
   b) the employment of women.
2. a) Why do you think Cobden's book (Source C) was called 'The White Slaves of England'?

   b) Write a short passage that might have appeared in the book.
3. What do Sources B and E tell us about working conditions in the 19th century? Are they equally reliable? Explain your answer.
4. What arguments are used in Source G against the employment of women? What does this tell us about male attitudes in the 19th century?

Reform and its effects

The arguments for reform did have an effect. Some factory owners did not wait for the law to change. They provided better working conditions voluntarily. Some of these 'voluntary reformers' set up model factories in the hope that other factory owners would follow their example.

But many owners of factories and mines did not agree that there was a need for change. Reformers found it difficult to persuade Parliament to pass new laws and when they were passed it was difficult to make them work.

Source A Voluntary reform at New Lanark, Scotland

The classroom at Robert Owen's 'model' factory. Owen paid good wages and limited working hours to 10.5 per day. He still made a profit and used it to build houses, shops and a school for the workers.

Source B Factory Acts

Between 1819 and 1874, Parliament passed a number of laws (Acts of Parliament) to help improve working conditions in factories. The table shows the maximum number of working hours allowed per day. The Acts passed before 1867 only concerned cotton factories.

Date of Act	Workers Affected	Terms of Act
1819	Under 18s	12 hours
1833	Children under 9	Banned from working
	Children aged 9-13	8 hours
	Children aged 13-18	12 hours
		Factory inspectors appointed
1844	Children aged 8-13	6.5 hours
	Children aged 13-18	12 hours
	Women	12 hours
		All machinery to be fenced
1847*	All children under 18	10 hours
	All women	10 hours
1850	All children under 18	10.5 hours
	All women	10.5 hours
In 1867 the terms of the Act passed in 1850 were extended to all factories.		
1874	All workers (including men)	10 hours
	Children under 10	Banned from working
	Children aged 10-14	Part-time work only

* This Act had to be replaced by the 1850 Act because factory owners ignored the 10 hour rule.

Source C

The best way of maintaining good behaviour was to use a 'silent monitor'. This was a four sided piece of wood, 2 inches long and 1 broad with each side coloured a different colour. It was hung near to each worker and the colour on the front indicated the conduct of the individual on the previous day. Bad was shown by black, indifferent by blue, good by yellow and excellent by white.

Robert Owen, 'The Life of Robert Owen', 1857

Source D Mines Acts

1842 No boys under age 10, girls or women allowed to work underground.

1853 Regular safety inspections to be made.

1860 No boys under age 12 allowed to work.

Source E

Complaints about reform, 1887

A group of women chainmakers went to protest against a proposal that they should not be allowed to do heavy work. They were worried that this would mean they could only do lower paid work.

The Home Secretary began to explain to the women that a medical officer had reported to him that the heavier hammers would damage their health, especially those of child bearing age. A very strong looking woman immediately said, 'I've had fourteen children, sir, and I never was better in my life'.

R. Strachey, 'The Cause', 1928

Source F A cartoon from 1871

A woman complains that she has already been working for 14 hours and has not yet finished.

Source G Inspection of a nail factory, 1864

Little boys and girls can be seen at work at the tip-punching machines with their fingers in constant danger of being punched off once in every second. 'They seldom lose a hand', said one of the owners, 'it only takes off a finger at the first or second joint. Sheer carelessness.'

Children's Employment Commission, Third Report, 1864

Source H Factory Inspectors

From 1833 factory inspectors were appointed to check that factory owners obeyed the new laws. At first only 4 inspectors were appointed to inspect all the factories in Britain. The usual fine for breaking the law was just £1.

Activities

1. Suppose it is 1833 and you have been asked to inspect cotton mills and write a report. Using Sources A, B and C compare New Lanark with other factories. Include interviews with workers.
2. What evidence is there in Sources B and D to show that working conditions had improved by 1900?
3. Using Sources E and F explain why some women thought reforms unhelpful.
4. Look at Sources G and H. Why do you think factory inspectors were appointed? What effect would you expect them to have on working conditions? Explain your answer.

Growth of trade unions

It was not only factory owners like Robert Owen who supported improvements in working conditions. The workers themselves began to demand changes through their trade unions. Even before Britain had become industrialised groups of workers had combined together to try to improve wages and working conditions. In the 19th century these groups developed into trade unions (groups of workers who worked in the same trade). At first employers tried to prevent workers from organising trade unions. It was easier to ignore complaints from individual workers than from large groups. But from the 1850s trade unions became better organised. Skilled workers formed national unions with full-time paid officials to run them efficiently.

Source A

In 1825, the Association of Colliers in the Rivers Tyne and Wear was set up. Miners joined it:

To make provision for themselves and families in case of death, sickness or accident and to unite in a firm manner in order to obtain more suitable pay and to reduce the hours of labour.

Robert Galloway, 'Annals of Coal Mining', 1898

Source B

Membership certificate of the Amalgamated Society of Woodworkers (ASW)

Source C

The Tolpuddle Martyrs

After reducing our pay to 7 shillings a week, our employers told us they must then lower it to 6 shillings. The working men met together to decide what must be done as they knew it was impossible to live honestly on such small means. I had read about trade societies. I told them of this and they willingly agreed to form a friendly society among the workers because they knew that any attempt to change the employers' decision on their own would be in vain.

George Loveless, 'The Victims of Whiggery', 1837

George Loveless and 5 other workers (the 'Tolpuddle Martyrs') were convicted of taking illegal oaths and sentenced to transportation for 7 years. After widespread protests, they were pardoned.

One way that workers can protest about working conditions is to go on strike (refuse to work). But strikes only succeed if all (or nearly all) the workers at a workplace refuse to work. Throughout the 19th century unions encouraged workers to join them. The more workers from a particular trade that joined, the greater the chance that employers would make improvements. Employers would listen to the union's demands if they knew that the union had the power to call a strike. In the late 19th century the unions organised a number of successful strikes. These strikes helped to improve working conditions.

Source D Cartoon from 1852

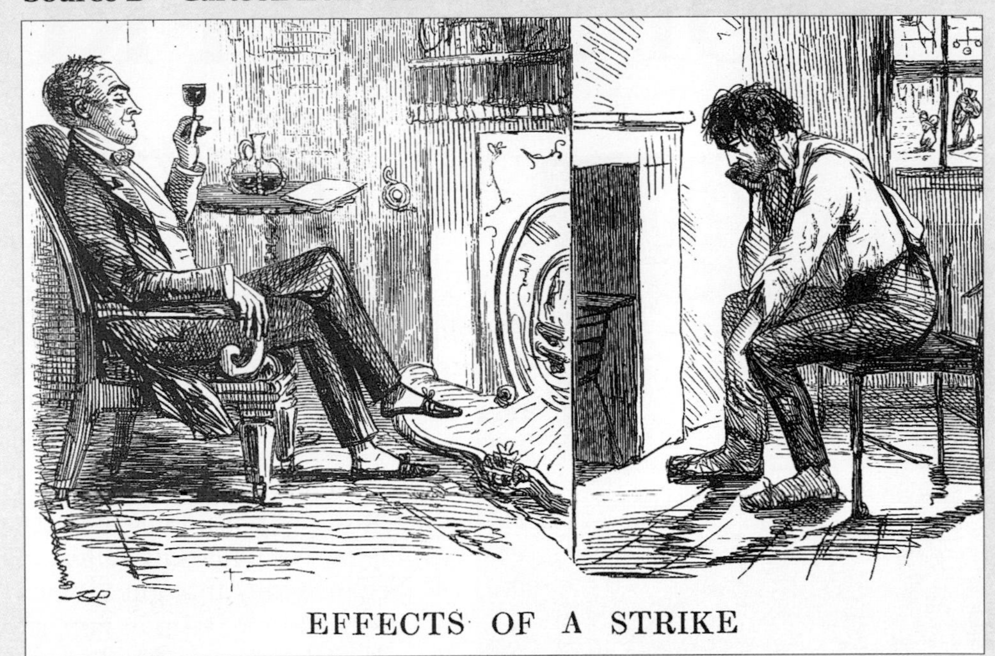

Although employers lost money during a strike because the workplace was shut, strikes were often hard for workers because they did not get paid and had to rely on money from the union.

Source E Dock strike, 1889

Every industry was paralysed. Tens of thousands of tons of food lay rotting in the ships in the Thames. The river was overcrowded with vessels unable to unload their cargo or go elsewhere. The tremendous influence of the Union of Dockers will give the workers faith in themselves. Everything is possible in the future for the toiling millions of the mine, the workshop and the factory.

'Reynolds News', September 1 1889

Checklist

- Conditions in the first factories and in mines were uncontrolled. Hours were long and few owners cared about the health and safety of their workers.
- From the early 19th century there was increasing concern about the employment of women and children.
- Working conditions improved slowly. Some improvements were made voluntarily, some by Acts of Parliament.
- Trade unions were set up to campaign for better pay and conditions. Sometimes strike action was taken.

Activities

1. Using Sources A and C make a list of the aims of trade unions.
2. Look at Source B. What does it tell us about the ASW? Devise a similar membership certificate for a school pupils' union.
3. Look at Sources D and E. Draw a chart showing the advantages and disadvantages of strikes to both workers and employers.
4. What do you think employers thought of unions? Support your arguments with evidence from these pages.

7 POPULAR PROTEST

The Brixton riots 1981. Some people claim that poverty was a major cause of these riots.

Protest at News International 1989. Printers feared new technology would threaten jobs.

March against the Poll Tax in 1991. Many people thought this tax was unfair.

Themes

Governments have never been able to please all of the people all of the time. When large numbers of people are discontented, they tend to join together to protest. Sometimes they protest peacefully. At other times they use violence. A violent protest is often called a riot.

When riots broke out in Bristol, Birmingham, London, Liverpool, Coventry and other cities during the early 1980s and 1990s, many people were shocked because they thought violent popular protests were unusual in Britain. In fact, riots - like peaceful protests - have been part of British political life for centuries.

In the 18th century there were riots over bread prices, taxation, wars and enclosures - even over the introduction of a new calendar. In the 19th century almost anything which changed the existing state of affairs could spark a protest.

This chapter looks at the following questions.

- What were the causes of popular discontent between 1750 and 1900?
- How did the protesters try to achieve their aims?
- How did people in power react to popular protest?

Focus Activities

1. It is the 1830s. You are a journalist from a newspaper which believes that it is right to hang rioters. Write an article about John Coulter. Include an interview with the Prime Minister, the Duke of Wellington.
2. Suppose that, on the night before he was hanged, John Coulter had written a brief history of his life. What might he have written?
3. Do you think that the person who drew these cartoons thought that John Coulter got what he deserved? Explain how you reached your answer.

The decline and fall of John Coulter

These cartoons were drawn between 1828 and 1830 when the Duke of Wellington was Prime Minister. They show what happened to an imaginary farm labourer called John Coulter.

John Coulter was easily satisfied. He lived a simple life as a farm labourer. He was happy as long as he and his family had enough to eat and clothes to wear.

In the late 1820s things went wrong. John lost his job and his home. He was forced to live off handouts from his local parish.

Thinking the government would help him, John asked the Prime Minister (the Duke of Wellington) for assistance. The Duke refused.

John was desperate. One night, he and some others decided they had suffered enough. They protested by smashing up the machines which had taken away their jobs.

Sadly for him, John was caught and put on trial. He was found guilty and sentenced to hang.

Causes of discontent

The Focus shows how John Coulter became so desperate that he joined a riot. Between 1790 and 1840 there were over 700 full-scale riots in Britain. These took place in both towns and the countryside and in many parts of Britain. The majority of rioters came from the poorer sections of society.

Source A The Luddites

New machines threatened jobs. Protest letters to factory owners were often signed 'Ned Ludd'. He was the mythical leader of the people who broke into factories to destroy machines. The machine breakers became known as 'Luddites'. This picture comes from a film about the Luddites.

Source B A meeting at a soup shop in Wigan

Into the meeting came a poor weaver.
'For three months', said he, 'myself, my wife and four children have not tasted an atom of flesh and we'll die every one of us before we accept charity and take your soup.'
'Well, honest fellow', said I, 'what do you want?'
'Want? Want?', he said, 'Why, I'm an Englishman. Give me my rights, I want no more.'

Henry Hunt's speech at a demonstration in London, 1816

Source C The Peterloo Massacre

In 18th century Britain, only a small number of men were allowed to vote. The French revolution of 1789 spread ideas about political equality and soon people in Britain with no vote began to protest. In 1819 a series of meetings was organised to demand changes to the voting system. In August a meeting was held in St Peter's Fields in Manchester. Events got out of hand. The local magistrates ordered soldiers to arrest the speakers and to break up the crowd. 11 people were killed and over 400 injured. This was known as 'Peterloo', a sarcastic reference to the battle of Waterloo of 1815. The heroic British victory over the French at Waterloo led to the end of a war which had begun in 1793.

Source D The Swing Riots

Changes in the countryside also caused hardship. New machines and enclosure meant fewer jobs. In the early 1830s there was a depression in farming and bread was expensive. There was rioting in the countryside. Protesters sent letters to landowners signed by 'Captain Swing', another mythical leader.

Source E Riots in 1842

It would appear that the riots began when, without warning, wages were reduced by one quarter. At once, with a desperation of purpose, people gathered in half-starved thousands and refused to work unless they could have 'a fair day's pay for a fair day's work'. All the manufacturing districts have been up in arms. At Stockport, where there are more than 20,000 persons unemployed, a large body of rioters broke open the workhouses and stole food and clothing whilst mobs robbed the shops.

'Illustrated London News', August 1842

Source F A comparison between the price of bread and the occurrence of riots

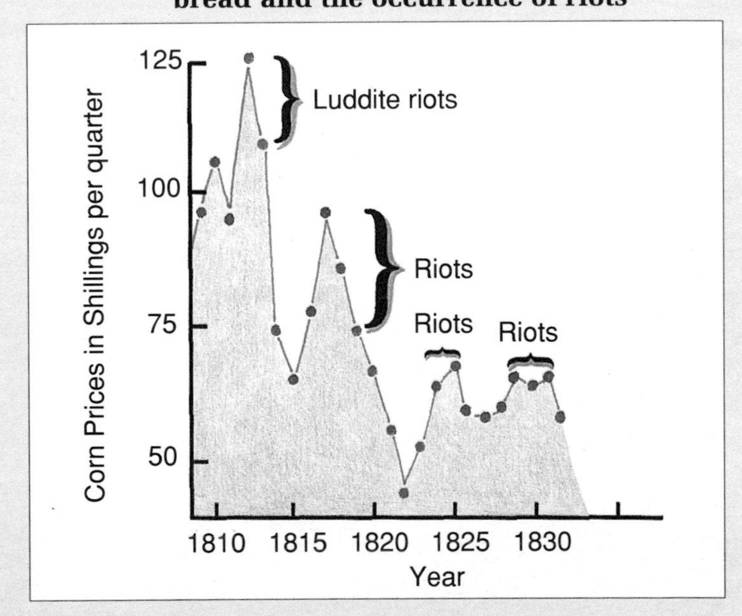

Activities

1. a) 'Ned Ludd' and 'Captain Swing' (Sources A and D) did not exist. Why do you think they were invented?

   b) Write a letter of protest from 'Ned Ludd' or 'Captain Swing'.

2. The weaver in Source B says 'Give me my rights'. Use the other sources to suggest what he might have meant by this.

3. What do Sources C, D, E and F tell us about the causes of popular discontent in the 19th century?

Tactics - the Chartists

Although riots were common in the first half of the 19th century, they did not achieve much. Factories continued to be built, machines were still used and few people were allowed to vote. However, rioting did draw attention to problems.

Violence was not the only tactic used by protesters. As the story of John Coulter in the Focus shows, it was a last resort - he only used it because other ways of solving his problems had failed. In fact some protesters thought that the use of violence was unhelpful. They used other tactics to try to achieve their goals.

In the late 1830s and 1840s the Chartist movement attracted the support of many thousands of working people across Britain. It was the first national protest movement and its tactics were designed to force changes to the political system.

The Chartists' campaign was based on a charter which demanded six reforms. Chartists believed that these reforms would make the British political system fairer.

Source A The Charter

The Six Points
OF THE
PEOPLE'S CHARTER.

1. A VOTE for every man twenty-one years of age, of sound mind, and not undergoing punishment for crime.

2. THE BALLOT.—To protect the elector in the exercise of his vote.

3. NO PROPERTY QUALIFICATION for Members of Parliament —thus enabling the constituencies to return the man of their choice, be he rich or poor.

4. PAYMENT OF MEMBERS, thus enabling an honest tradesman, working man, or other person, to serve a constituency, when taken from his business to attend to the interests of the country.

5. EQUAL CONSTITUENCIES, securing the same amount of representation for the same number of electors, instead of allowing small constituencies to swamp the votes of large ones.

6. ANNUAL PARLIAMENTS, thus presenting the most effectual check to bribery and intimidation, since though a constituency might be bought once in seven years (even with the ballot), no purse could buy a constituency (under a system of universal suffrage) in each ensuing twelvemonth; and since members, when elected for a year only, would not be able to defy and betray their constituents as now.

Source B Petitions: the second Chartist petition being taken to Parliament

In 1839, 1842 and 1848 the Chartists presented huge petitions (lists of supporters) to Parliament to back up their demands. They claimed that the first petition contained 1 million signatures, the second 3 million and the third 6 million. Opponents said they contained many fewer signatures and that they included false names, such as 'Mr Punch', 'Victoria Rex' and 'No Cheese'. Parliament rejected all three petitions.

Source C **Mass meetings: Chartists meet at Kennington Common, London 1848**

The Chartists set up local groups and held meetings to gain support. In 1848 a meeting of Chartists from all over the country was held on Kennington Common to march with the third petition to Parliament. The government appointed 150,000 special constables and banned the march, worried that this might be the start of a revolution. Fearing bloodshed, the Chartist leaders called off the march. It was clear that the government would not listen to Chartist demands and the movement collapsed.

Source D **The mass media**

16 Gt. Windmill Stre

The Northern Star,

AND NATIONAL TRADES' JOURNAL.

VOL. XI. No 565. LONDON, SATURDAY, AUGUST 19, 1848. PRICE FIVEPENCE or Five Shillings and Sixpence per Quarter

the timber paid for, the slates paid for, the ironmongery paid for, and all materials paid for.

No. 2—On the most favourable calculation the whole of the subscribers cannot possibly be located in less time than a period intermediate between 150 and 225 years.

Why, Fonblanque, you beat both Grey and Finlayson in the magic art of dissolving: in the least favourable view—that is, if these who expect benefit had paid up their shares in full—I would, without any additional contributions, or without the Bank, locate them all in ten years.

No. 3—The estimated produce appears from the evidence of a practical agriculturist to be in excess of what

for £90,714 1s. 1d. of subscriptions, and £4,222 7s. 2d. of extra contributions towards expenses of management!

Why, you incomprehensible ass, Finlayson with his magnifying glasses could not see through this mist. Just see what you do—you first reduce the value of property from 90,000*l.* to 60,000*l.*; then if I purchase 28,000*l.* more, you reduce the 60,000*l.* to 32,000*l.*, so that if I purchase 35,000*l.* worth more, you will make us 3,000*l.* worse than bankrupts. So that, Fonblanque, in point of fact, every fresh estate purchased diminishes the value of the former property, by the amount given for the new purchase. Out upon you, you snivelling tool,

the Land Company, the Bank, and the Chartist organisation, are all of them parts of Mr O'Connor's stock-in-trade. Together, they constitute the business by which he has for some years maintained himself. He makes the one play into the other. That by this means he has made his newspaper pay him £4,000 to £5,000 per annum is admitted; but what any other parties (except his immediate agents) have gained, is not so obvious. We are curious to know how long the gullibility of Mr O'Connor's followers and believers will enable him to carry on so thriving a trade.

Yes, you prostitute, it is apparent from the accounts of the "*Northern Star*," but from no other accounts, that Mr O'Connor has sustained the political movement and Whig victims at his own expense—but it is not apparent from the accounts of the Land Company, that

Colonial and Foreign.

THE FRENCH REPUBLIC.

THE LAW ON THE PRESS.

Paris, Thursday.—The project of law put forward by the government, in spite of an obstinate and animated resistance from the ultra-democrats and members of the Mountain, led by M. Ledru Rollin, and brought up in the rear by M. Flocon, was adopted by a majority of 497 against 342. The duration of the law at present voted is limited to the 1st of May next, in which interval it is expected that the legislature will establish a permanent system of laws to regulate the press.

THE JUNE INSURRECTION—FATE OF THE PRISONERS.

The Chartists published their own newspaper, the 'Northern Star'. In 1839, this newspaper sold 60,000 copies per week.

Source E **Leadership**

Some Chartists believed in 'moral' force - peaceful methods. Others supported 'physical' force - the use of violence to achieve their ends.

No other means are likely to be so effective as a peaceful combination of the millions.
W. Lovett and J. Collins, 1840

Nobody can doubt that O'Brien (a Chartist leader) has little faith in a peaceful campaign and that he looks to a revolution to overthrow the present government We do not believe that the people will ever be got to act in sufficient numbers to gain it by violence.
The 'True Scotsman', July 1839

Activities

1. Take each of the 6 points in Source A and explain what the Chartists thought was wrong with the existing political system.
2. a) Using Sources B, C, D and E explain how the Chartists tried to achieve their aims and why their leaders were divided about tactics.

   b) Write an article for the 'Northern Star' which explains which tactics would succeed and why.
3. Write your own 'Pupils' Charter' and describe the tactics you might use to persuade the government to lower the voting age to 14.

Controlling the mob

Until the 1830s the only way to control riots or to break up mass demonstrations was to use soldiers. But their presence often inflamed the crowd and resulted in bloodshed. Soldiers were only called as a last resort. It was not their job to prevent crowds from gathering or riots from starting.

The Gordon Riots of June 1780 lasted a fortnight and 700 people were killed. After this some people began to demand a permanent non-military police force whose job would be to catch criminals and deal with public disorder. Opponents argued that the daily presence of police constables would destroy privacy and freedom. However, after helping to set up a successful (but rather brutal) police force in Ireland, Robert Peel brought his ideas to the mainland. In 1829, 3,000 police constables were recruited in London. In 1856 a law was passed requiring every borough and county in Britain to set up its own police force.

Source A   A riot in Bristol, 1831

Although a police force was set up in London in 1829, many areas still relied on soldiers until 1856. People were often killed when soldiers were called in to deal with riots.

Source B   The new police force

Liberty or death! Britons! Honest men! The time has at last arrived. We assure you that 6,000 cutlasses (swords) have been removed from the Tower of London for the use of Peel's Bloody Gang. These damned Police are now to be armed. Englishmen, will you put up with this?

Anonymous leaflet produced in the 1830s

Source C   A 'Peeler'

The new police constables were known as 'Bobbies' or 'Peelers' after their founder, Robert Peel. They were organised into divisions and paid a wage. A top hat reinforced with metal completed a blue uniform (soldiers wore red). Constables were armed with wooden truncheons whilst officers had pistols. They were provided with swords only in times of crisis.

Source D Instructions to police constables

June 3, 1830. The police constable is not authorised to arrest anyone without being able to prove that a law has been broken. No constable is to arrest anyone for words only. Language, however violent, towards a police constable is not to be noticed.

August 21, 1830. Constables are to remember that they are required to do their duty with good temper and discretion. Any instance of unnecessary violence by them will be severely punished.

'General Instructions for Constables', issued by the Metropolitan Police Commissioners, 1830

Source E Opposition to the police, 1855

A View of the Brutal Attack
ON AN UNARMED, RESPECTABLE, AND PEACEABLE MULTITUDE
OF BOTH SEXES, AND ALL AGES, MADE BY A
DESPOTIC POLICE,
IN HYDE PARK, ON SUNDAY, JULY 1st, 1855
DEDICATED TO LORD G———R AND ALL THE SAINTS,

Source F Success of the new police

The large reduction in the amount of crime committed soon became sufficient to remove the feelings against the new force and to make it popular with the public.

J. Grant, 1838

Checklist

- Changes in living and working conditions, poverty and the demand for reform of the political system were all causes of popular protest between 1750 and 1900.
- Although protests were often violent, peaceful tactics were sometimes used. The Chartists tried to win political reform by publicising their demands to gain mass support.
- People in power responded to popular protest by introducing a permanent police force. The job of the police was to reduce crime and to control crowds.

Activities

1. a) Using Sources A and B give the arguments for and against setting up a new police force.
   b) What do Sources C, E and F tell us about attitudes towards the early police force?
2. Using Sources C and D draw a poster advertising for new recruits to the police force and write a letter of application for the job of police constable.
3. Compare Source A with Source E. How did crowd control change after the police force was set up?

8 POLITICS

George II 1727-60

George III 1760-1820

George IV 1820-30

William IV 1830-37

Victoria 1837-1901

Themes

Today we take it for granted that people over the age of 18 should be able to choose their local Member of Parliament (MP) by voting in a Parliamentary election. We expect elections to be fair. We would be shocked, for example, to hear that candidates in an election had bribed people to vote for them. But it is only in the 20th century that the majority of people have been given the right to vote. In 1750 less than 5% of adults were allowed to vote. Bribery and corruption were common. The MPs who were elected to the House of Commons did not represent the population as a whole. They represented only a small section of the population.

The changes that took place in British society between 1750 and 1900 brought new problems and new demands. One demand was for changes to be made to the electoral system. Electoral reform became one of several important political issues to concern the government and people during this period.

This chapter looks at these questions.

- How did the British political system change between 1750 and 1900?
- What were the key political issues during this period?

Focus Activities

1. Would you describe the election on the Focus page as 'fair'? Explain your answer.
2. Why do you think the final result of the election differed from the result at the meeting on 10 December?
3. What does the picture on the Focus page tell us about elections in the early 19th century?
4. List the ways in which the election described on the Focus page differs from elections today.

An election in London, December 1832

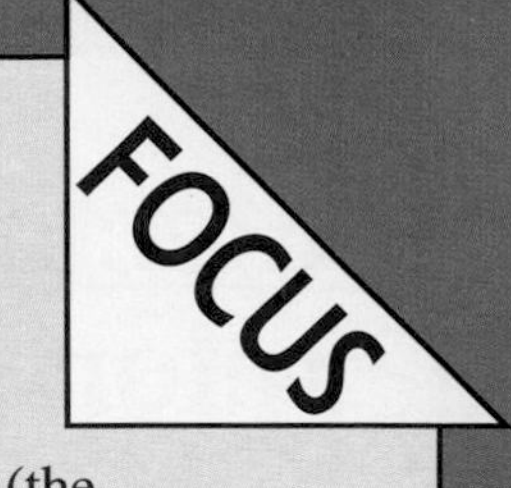

In the early 19th century elections were 'open'. When an election was announced a large wooden platform (the 'hustings') was built in a public place. Candidates made speeches from the platform and then the voters were asked to vote by a show of hands. No women and only some men were allowed to vote. If the vote between two candidates was close, a 'poll' could be demanded. Each voter would have to go up on to the platform and prove he had a vote. He would then have to state publicly which candidate he supported. Often voters would be bribed to support a particular candidate. It was common for landlords who stood as candidates to threaten to evict their tenants if they did not vote for them. The passage below describes an election in 1832.

The election for the borough of Finsbury took place on Islington Green. On Friday 10 December the clerk came forward and asked all those who were not allowed to vote to depart from the Green. Refusal to obey would mean prison. But, as usual, no one paid any attention to the command. The clerk then asked the voters for a show of hands. He read out the name of a candidate and asked that candidate's supporters to raise their hands. He then read out the next name and so on. A reasonable number of hands appeared for Mr Babbage, a greater number for Mr Temple, about the same number for Mr Grant, a very few for Mr Spankie and a great number for Mr Wakeley. It is only fair to state that many boys and others who certainly could not be voters held up their hands. The Returning Officer (the official in charge of the election) declared that Mr Wakeley and Mr Grant had been elected. Uproar followed this announcement. Many in the crowd claimed that Mr Temple had a larger show of hands than Mr Grant. Three candidates - Mr Babbage, Mr Temple and Mr Spankie - then demanded a poll. The Returning Officer agreed to this. The result of the poll was declared on Wednesday 15 December. The result was as follows:

Mr Grant	4278	Mr Wakeley	2151
Mr Spankie	2848	Mr Temple	787
Mr Babbage	2311		

The Returning Officer announced, amidst cheers and some groaning from the crowd, that Mr Grant and Mr Spankie had been duly elected.

'The Observer', December 1832

Electoral reform

In the General Election held in April 1992 over 32 million people voted. Today Britain is divided into 651 roughly equal constituencies (voting areas). In each constituency one MP is elected to Parliament. Over 99% of people over the age of 18 are allowed to vote in a General Election.

Before 1832 less than 5% of the adult population was allowed to vote. The right to vote depended on a property qualification (a man had to own property worth a certain value to be allowed to vote). Also, Britain was divided into two types of constituency - counties (voters in each county elected two MPs) and boroughs (voters in each borough elected two MPs). The number of voters in these constituencies varied widely - some had several thousand voters whilst others had less than fifty.

Unlike today, elections were 'open' - voters had to declare their choice in public. Also they did not all vote on the same day. Before 1832 elections sometimes lasted for as long as a fortnight.

Source A The electoral system in the early 19th century

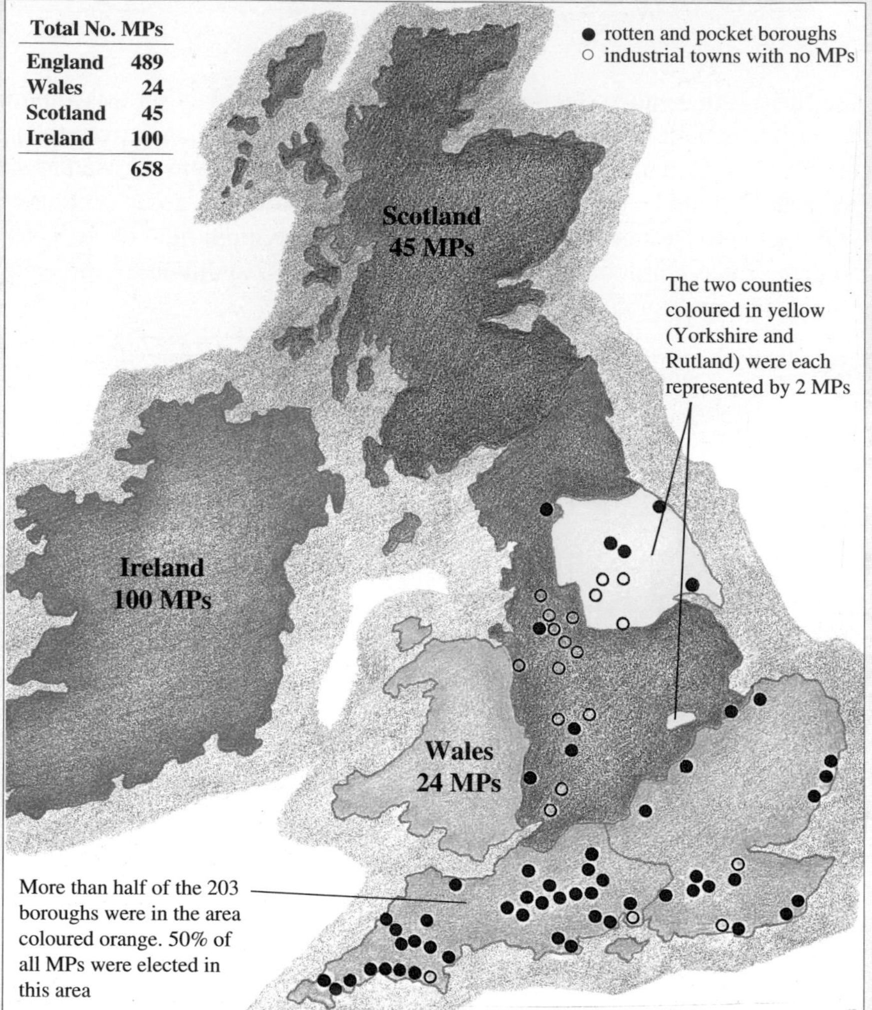

Constituencies with populations small enough for voters to be bribed were known as 'pocket boroughs' (because an MP who bribed the voters had them 'in his pocket'). Constituencies with populations so small that there were only a handful of voters were known as 'rotten boroughs'. In one rotten borough called Old Sarum there were only 7 voters. In contrast many of the new industrial towns did not have their own MPs to represent them.

Source B

The county of Yorkshire which contains nearly a million people sends two county MPs to Parliament - and so does the county of Rutland which contains not a hundredth part of that number. The town of Old Sarum which contains three houses sends two MPs to Parliament and the town of Manchester (which has a population of over 60,000) is not allowed to send any.

Thomas Paine, 'Rights of Man', 1791

Source C

We don't now live in the days of Barons. We live in the days of Leeds, of Bradford, of Halifax, of Huddersfield. We live in days when men are industrious and desire to be free. I am for extending the rights of voting in the great towns of England. I go a great deal further. I am for extending the right of voting to that class of people who have no right now in any town in England - every householder. In other words, every man who lives in a house and pays rates.

Henry Brougham, election speech made in July 1830

Source D The House of Lords and the 'Great' Reform Act, 1831-32

Today if a Bill (a proposal) is passed by the House of Commons three times it becomes law even if the House of Lords votes against it. But in the 19th century if the Lords voted against a Bill then it could not become law. In 1831 the government proposed a new electoral law. It was passed by the Commons but rejected by the Lords. In March 1832 the Prime Minister, Earl Grey, reintroduced the Bill. The Lords threatened to reject it again. But Grey persuaded the King, William IV, to promise to appoint a large number of supporters of electoral reform to the House of Lords if the Bill was not passed (Lords are not elected, they are appointed by the Monarch). The Lords passed the Bill.

Source E Electoral reform 1800-85

1832 First 'Great' Reform Act
New constituencies: 56 rotten boroughs were abolished (they had elected 112 MPs) and 30 boroughs with a population under 4,000 elected 1 rather than 2 MPs. 142 MPs were now elected by voters in industrial towns.
Property qualification: reduced and made more uniform.
Number of voters: rose by 200,000.

1867 Second Reform Act
New constituencies: 45 boroughs with a population under 10,000 elected 1 rather than 2 MPs. 45 extra MPs were now elected by voters in industrial towns and London.
Property qualification: all male householders in the boroughs could vote. Qualifications for county elections remained (though at a reduced level).
Number of voters: rose by 1 million.

1872 Secret Ballot Act
No more 'open' elections - people to vote in secret.

1883 Corrupt Practices Act
Election expenses for candidates standardised and bribery and corruption punished.

1884/85 Third Reform Act
New constituencies: 1 MP for each constituency. Boroughs with a population under 15,000 abolished and new constituencies with larger populations created.
Property qualification: all male householders could vote in counties and boroughs.
Number of voters: rose by over 2 million.

Source F Percentage of adults (over age 21) allowed to vote, 1831-1928

Date	%	Date	%
1831	5	1884	28.5
1833	7	1918	74
1867	16	1928	97

Activities

1. Using Sources A, B and C explain why there was a need for electoral reform in the early 19th century.
2. Look at Source D. Suppose you were a journalist in 1831-32. Write an article explaining the difficulties faced by the government in passing the 'Great' Reform Act.
3. Look at Sources E and F.
   a) Why do you think the First Reform Act is known as the 'Great' Reform Act?
   b) Describe how the electoral system changed in the 19th century.
   c) Would you say that the changes were 'rapid' or 'gradual'? Explain your answer.

The effects of reform

Electoral reform in the 19th century meant great political change. One result was the development of modern political parties. The old parties - the Whigs (later Liberals) and Tories (later Conservatives) - had to become better organised to win over the new voters. A second result was the creation of the Labour Party. By the late 19th century many workers had the vote. The Labour Party was created to represent their interests. A third result was the growing demand that women should be allowed to vote.

Source A Election result in Shrewsbury, 1857

The candidates made their speeches on Friday at the hustings set up in front of St Chad's Church. A large group of roughs assembled there to annoy the Conservative candidates. The poll opened on Saturday morning at 8 am and closed at 4 pm. The Mayor declared the result as follows:

Mr Tomline	Liberal	706
Mr Slaney	Liberal	695
Mr Huddleston	Conservative	548
Major Phibbs	Conservative	484

Mr Tomline and Mr Slaney were duly elected as Members of Parliament.

'Shrewbury Journal', 3 April 1857

Source B Election result in Shrewsbury, 1874

The election of two members to represent this borough took place yesterday. There was very little of the excitement of earlier elections. In the afternoon the voters came up 'few and far between' and the clerks had little difficulty checking them off. At 4 pm the voting booths (rooms where people could make their vote in private) were closed and the voters went to the Market Square to wait for the announcement. The crowd waited patiently until the result was posted up. The result was as follows:

Mr Cotes	Liberal	1672
Mr Robertson	Liberal	1561
Mr Figgins	Conservative	1388
Mr Straight	Conservative	1328

Mr Cotes and Mr Robertson were duly elected as Members of Parliament.

'Shrewsbury Journal', 4 February 1874

Source C Election result in Shrewsbury, 1885

By the biggest majority of votes ever known in this borough, Mr Watson triumphed. The Conservative Party was united whilst the Liberal Party was not. Also, Mr Watson was a well known neighbour whereas the Liberal was a little known stranger. The counting of the vote began on Friday morning at 8am. At 9am the result was declared as follows:

Mr Watson	Conservative	2244
Mr Waring	Liberal	1512

Mr Watson was duly elected as member of Parliament.

'Shrewsbury Chronicle', 4 December 1885

Source D

BOROUGH AND COUNTY

ELECTIONS.

MESSRS. DENTON AND GRAY

Intimate to their Workmen that they are at perfect liberty to Vote for any Candidate they please, and that the side they take in Politics will not in any way affect their employment.

Middleton Ship Yard,
Hartlepool, June 23rd, 1868.

Hartlepool: J. Procter, Printer and Lithographer by Steam Power. 11,745.

This poster was produced by the owners of a shipyard in 1868

Source E Election result in Shrewsbury and Atcham, 1992

Electorate		70,602
Derek Conway	Conservative	26,681
Kenneth Hemsley	Liberal Democrat	15,716
Liz Owen	Labour	15,157
Geoff Hardy	Green	677

Turnout was 82.45% of the total electorate.

'The Guardian', 11 April 1992

Source F Political parties

Electoral reform meant that political parties needed to find new ways to win support for their candidates. In 1879 William Gladstone, leader of the Liberal party, went on a campaign in Midlothian, Scotland to win votes for Liberal candidates there. This was the first modern style election campaign.

Many of the new voters, however, did not share the aims of the old parties. The Reform Acts of 1867 and 1884 gave the vote to many workers. In 1893 a new political party was set up to represent the interests of workers – the Independent Labour Party (ILP). The picture (left) is an ILP membership certificate. It has been signed by one of the ILP's founding members and first MP, Keir Hardie. When the trade unions agreed to support the ILP in 1900 it became the Labour Party.

Source G Women and the vote

Electoral reform meant that more and more men were given the vote. But women's demands for the vote were ignored. Towards the end of the 19th century women began to campaign to change this. Women who supported this campaign became known as 'Suffragettes' ('suffrage' means 'the vote'). In 1888 women won the right to vote in local elections. In 1918 women over the age of 30 were allowed to vote in General Elections. In 1928 women's voting age was lowered to 21 (the same as men).

Activities

1. a) Using Sources A, B and C describe how elections changed between 1850 and 1885.
   b) What does Source E tell us about changes in elections since 1885?
2. Why do you think the poster in Source D was put up? What does it tell us about elections at this time?
3. Look at Source F.
   a) Why did political parties need to be better organised by 1900?
   b) How would you expect the new Labour Party to affect election results? Explain your answer.
4. Suppose the picture in Source G had appeared in a leaflet arguing for the vote for women. Write down the arguments that might have been used in the leaflet.

Women's rights

Is your teacher a man or a woman? What about your doctor or your local MP? Today women and men have equal rights under the law. But this is a recent development. In the 19th century women were second class citizens with few rights. A man could legally imprison his wife or take her children away from her. Until 1882 a married woman's property belonged to her husband. There was little opportunity for the education or training of women.

It was difficult for women to change this because they had no say in the government of the country. They could not vote and were not allowed to stand for election as MPs. By 1900, however, the idea that women should have equal rights with men was becoming an important political issue.

Source A Education

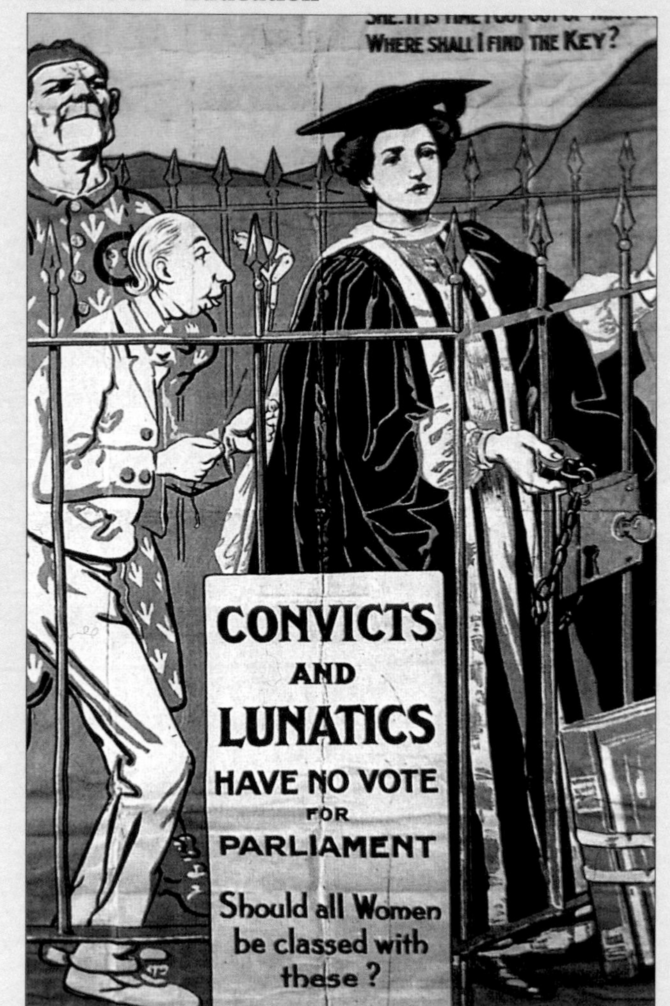

Before the 1850s few girls received more than a basic education (reading and writing). Men educated their sons but argued that girls only needed to learn how to look after the house and care for a family. Some women, however, realised that education would give women a better chance of gaining equality. In the 1850s new schools were set up for girls. They followed a curriculum similar to that of boys' schools and charged reasonable fees (still too high for poor families). Many Suffragettes were educated women.

Source B Advice to women in the 1880s

The mere act of riding a bicycle is not in itself sinful and if it is the only way of reaching the church on Sunday it may be excusable. On the other hand, if walking or riding in the usual way is discarded for the sake of the exercise or thrill bicycle riding brings, it is clearly wrong.

'Home Companion', 1885

Source C

There is a new dawn, a dawn of freedom and it is brought about by the cycle. Free to spin into the glorious country without a chaperone (an older companion), the young girl of today can feel the real independence of herself.

Louise Jey, 1895

Source D The motor car

New forms of transport gave women the opportunity to be more independent - if they could afford them.

Source E The first women doctors

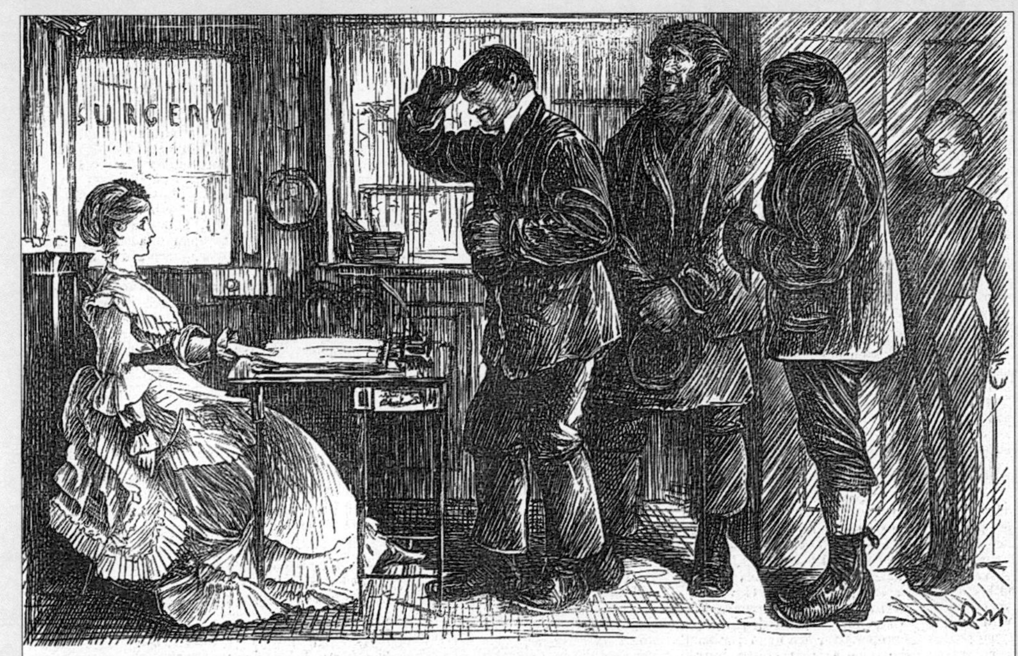

OUR PRETTY DOCTOR.

Dr. Arabella. "WELL, MY GOOD FRIENDS, WHAT CAN I DO FOR YOU?"
Bill. "WELL, MISS, IT'S ALL ALONG O' ME AND MY MATES BEIN' OUT O' WORK, YER SEE, AND WANTIN' TO TURN AN HONEST PENNY HANYWAYS WE CAN; SO, 'AVIN' 'EARD TELL AS *YOU* WAS A RISIN' YOUNG MEDICAL PRACTITIONER, WE THOUGHT AS P'RAPS YOU WOULDN'T MIND JUST A RECOMMENDIN' OF *HUS* AS NURSES."

In 1865, after a determined struggle, Elizabeth Garrett qualified as a medical practitioner (doctor). She was the first British woman to gain this qualification. Before then women had only been allowed to be nurses. Doctors make the important decisions about patients. Nurses carry out the treatment doctors prescribe.

With the example and encouragement of Dr Garrett, women were soon able to prove that they were as able as men in the field of medicine. However, there was still a great deal of prejudice against them.

Source F

I was born in Bethnal Green on 9 April 1855. I was my mother's seventh child and seven more were born after me – which made my mother a perfect slave. Generally speaking she was either expecting a baby to be born or had one at the breast. When there were eight of us, the oldest was not big enough to get ready to go to school without help.

Mrs Layton, 'Memories of Seventy Years' in M. Llewelyn Davies, 'Life As We Have Known It', 1931

Source G Birth control

Population statistics suggest that after the 1870s middle class people began to use contraception. These figures from London contrast the birth rate in Hampstead, a middle class area, with working class Shoreditch.

Year	Place	Births*	Year	Place	Births*
1881	Hampstead	31.2	1911	Hampstead	17.5
	Shoreditch	30.0		Shoreditch	30.2

*The figures show the number of births per 1,000 people.

The few people who campaigned for birth control were rebels. In 1877 Annie Besant and Charles Bradlaugh were arrested for publishing a book on birth control. It was banned and described as a 'filthy dirty book'. Their trial was given much publicity and several thousand copies were sold.

Carol Adams, 'Ordinary Lives', 1982

Activities

1. Look at the sources on these pages. What evidence is there that life improved for some women in the 19th century but for others there was little improvement?
2. Would you say that the author of Source B and the cartoonist who drew Source E supported women's equality with men? Explain your answer.
3. 'Women's struggle for equality was more than a struggle for the vote.' Explain this statement using the sources on these pages.

Free trade and protection

Suppose you had gone into a shop in Britain in 1750 to buy a loaf of bread. There were just two loaves left - one made with British flour and one made with French flour. The loaf made with British flour would be cheaper. The reason for this is that in 1750 the British government 'protected' British trade from foreign competition by putting taxes (or 'duties') on all goods that came to Britain from abroad. So when foreign goods were sold in British shops the price of the foreign goods included the tax paid to the British government. This usually meant that the price of the foreign goods was higher than the price of the same goods produced in Britain. It also meant that the government earned more money from the taxes paid on the foreign goods.

The problem with this system of protection was that other countries also protected their own trade by charging a tax on British goods which were sold abroad. Suppose you had visited France in 1750, for example, and saw two loaves similar to those you had seen above. The loaf made with French flour would be cheaper than the loaf made with British flour.

Throughout the 19th and 20th centuries arguments have raged about whether there should be taxes on foreign goods or whether trade should be free. Between 1750 and 1900 the 'free trade' debate was a key political issue.

Source A Free trade

A medallion commemorating 'The Wealth of Nations'

In 1776 the economist Adam Smith published a book called 'The Wealth of Nations'. This book argued that there was no need to tax foreign goods because that prevented free competition between countries. Since Britain was the first industrial nation it was able to produce more goods more cheaply than other countries. Free trade would therefore benefit Britain because more British produced goods could be sold abroad.

Source B A free trade hat

Free trade was not possible whilst the Corn Laws remained in force. Passed in 1815 to protect British farmers from bankruptcy, these laws kept foreign corn out of Britain until the price of British corn reached 80 shillings per quarter ton. This made sure that the price of bread remained high. Opponents said that these laws stopped foreign countries buying goods produced in Britain. They were repealed (abolished) in 1846 and by the 1860s Britain was a free trading nation. This picture comes from the inside of a hat made by Mr Marriot, a hatter who supported free trade.

Source C **A poster showing the hazards of free trade, 1906**

From the 1870s newly industrialised countries (such as Germany and the USA) were able to export more goods than Britain. Free trade no longer seemed so attractive. There was less demand for British goods and some foreign goods sold in Britain were cheaper than British produced goods. Some people began to argue for a return to protection. For example, Joseph Chamberlain proposed a scheme of 'imperial preference'. Goods from the Empire, he said, should not be taxed whilst those from other countries should be. This idea was rejected. His opponents feared that protection would mean less choice and higher prices.

Source D **The flag of the European Community**

Arguments about free trade continue today. Since 1973 Britain has been a member of the the European Community. One of the aims of the European Community is to encourage free trade between its members. In 1987 the 'Single European Act' was passed. This Act contains a clause which states that the European Community is to be, 'an area in which the free movement of goods, persons and services is ensured'.

Source E

We believe that free trade will increase the demand for labour of every kind – for the mechanical classes and labourers, for clerks, shopkeepers and people who work in warehouses. We also believe that free trade will not reduce, but on the contrary will increase, the nation's revenue since the government will gain more money from taxes.

Speech made by Richard Cobden, July 1844

Activities

1. It is 1844. Use Sources A, B and E to produce a leaflet in support of free trade. Explain in the leaflet what is meant by free trade and why it would benefit Britain.
2. Look at Sources A and C. Suppose you had been able to interview Adam Smith and Joseph Chamberlain about the arguments for and against free trade. Write down the interviews and explain how their arguments depended on the times in which they lived.
3. What point do you think is being made by the poster in Source C?
4. Look at Source D. What do you think (a) a supporter of free trade and (b) a supporter of protection would think of the European Community today? Explain your answer.

Ireland

In 1750 Ireland was, in effect, a British colony. As in other British colonies the native population (the Catholics) had no political rights whilst the colonists (the Protestants) enjoyed many privileges. Ireland was different from other colonies, however, because it was so close to mainland Britain and because the colonists had lived there for much longer than in other British colonies.

In 1796 whilst Britain was at war with France, the French encouraged the Irish to unite against Britain. An attempted rebellion failed but it scared the British. In 1800 the British Parliament passed the Act of Union, making Ireland part of Great Britain for the first time. Ireland was given 100 seats in the House of Commons. But the Irish people were not asked whether they wanted Ireland to become part of Great Britain. As a result, the 'Irish Question' (the question of whether Ireland should remain part of Britain or become independent) remained a key political issue throughout the 19th century.

Source A The potato famine and its effects, 1845-49

A family about to be evicted from their home during the potato famine

Most land in Ireland was owned by Protestant colonists or English absentee landowners. They rented it out to tenant farmers (most of whom were Catholics). Many of these farmers lived entirely on potatoes which they grew themselves - they could not even afford bread. In 1845 disease struck the potato crop and it was soon clear that there would be a disaster unless action was taken. In 1841 the population of Ireland was just over 8 million. During the famine nearly 1 million people died from starvation and disease and over 2 million emigrated. This experience caused much bitterness.

Source B

The only way to prevent people from becoming habitually dependent on the government is to stop the sale of corn from government depots. The uncertainty about the new potato crop only makes it more necessary. Whatever may be done later, this must be stopped now or you run the risk of paralysing all private enterprise and making Ireland a burden on you for an indefinite number of years.

C. Trevelyan (Head of the British Treasury), letter written in July 1846

Source C

When the Queen at her Coronation swore to protect and defend her subjects, no exception was made with regard to Ireland. How does it happen then that while there is a shilling in the Treasury or even a jewel in the Crown that patient subjects are allowed to perish with hunger?

'Cork Examiner', 2 November 1846

Source D The Unionists

Although much of Ireland remained underdeveloped, Ulster (in the North) did not. The majority of people in Ulster were Protestants and they benefited from the industrial revolution. New industries grew up around Belfast. When people in Southern Ireland began, in the 1860s, to demand independence or 'Home Rule' many Protestants in Ulster opposed this demand. They did not want to be ruled by the Catholics in the South. They supported the Act of Union and wanted to remain British.

Source E The Nationalists

Although the Catholics gained equal political rights with Protestants in 1829, the British electoral laws meant that most could not vote. The failure of the British government to prevent the famine and to solve the problems faced by small farmers (high rents and eviction) led to growing demands for Home Rule. Different tactics were used by different groups. In the 1870s the Irish Land League organised boycotts and rent strikes. Other groups such as the Fenians (the 19th century version of the IRA) used violence. Nationalists wanted Ireland to be completely independent from Britain. This recent picture shows that support for Nationalism continues.

Activities

1. Suppose you were a tenant farmer who survived the potato famine. Using Sources A, B and C describe what happened and what you think about the government's policy towards the famine.
2. What do Sources D and E tell us about the attitude of (a) Unionists and (b) Nationalists towards the British government?
3. Using the sources on these pages explain why the 'Irish Question' remained a key political issue throughout the 19th century.

Checklist

- Between 1832 and 1900 electoral reform brought fairer elections. More men but no women were given the vote.
- Political parties became more organised. The Labour Party was set up to represent the interests of the new voters.
- Women's struggle for equality, free trade and protection and the 'Irish Question' were key political issues.

9 RELIGION AND MORALITY

This church has been converted into a radio station because the number of church-goers has declined.

Pumping iron for Jesus. Many religious groups today use modern techniques to win converts.

Themes

How religious are you? In Britain today most people say that they believe in God but less than a fifth of the population regularly goes to a religious service. A 1990 survey shows that of the 9 million adult church members, 1.8 million belonged to the Anglican Church (Church of England), 1.9 million were Catholics, 3.4 million belonged to other Christian churches and 1.9 million belonged to non-Christian groups.

In 1750 the majority of church-goers were Anglicans. Although membership of other religious groups was not banned, the Anglican Church had a special position - for example only Anglicans were allowed to stand for election to Parliament or hold public office.

By 1900, however, this had changed. Britain had become an industrial nation. The growth of industry brought a new way of life. As society changed so did the organisation and practice of religion.

The growth of industry also brought problems - such as poverty, lack of education and poor working conditions. Many of the people who tried to find solutions to these problems were Christians. Their beliefs influenced the sorts of solutions that they came up with.

This chapter looks at the following questions.

- How did the organisation and practice of religion change?
- How did Christian beliefs affect reform?
- What do we mean by 'Victorian values'?

Focus Activities

1. Use the Focus to make a table listing what William Booth thought were:
   a) the problems in British society
   b) the solutions to these problems.
2. How did Booth think that religion would help to achieve his aims?
3. a) Make a similar table of what you think are the most serious problems today. How would you solve them? How might religion help?
   b) Draw a modern version of the poster in the Focus to illustrate your table.

Source D The Religious Census of 1851

Population (England & Wales)	17 927 609
Possible worshippers*	12 549 326
Actual worshippers	7 261 032
Churches attended	
Church of England	3 773 474
Scottish Presbyterians	60 131
Independents	792 142
Baptists	587 978
Quakers	18 172
Methodists	1 325 382
Welsh Methodists	151 046
Catholics	305 393
Mormons	18 800
Jews	4 150
Others	224 364

* 30% of the population was estimated to be unable to attend Church on census day due to age, illness or work.

Census of Great Britain, 1851

Source E Charles Darwin

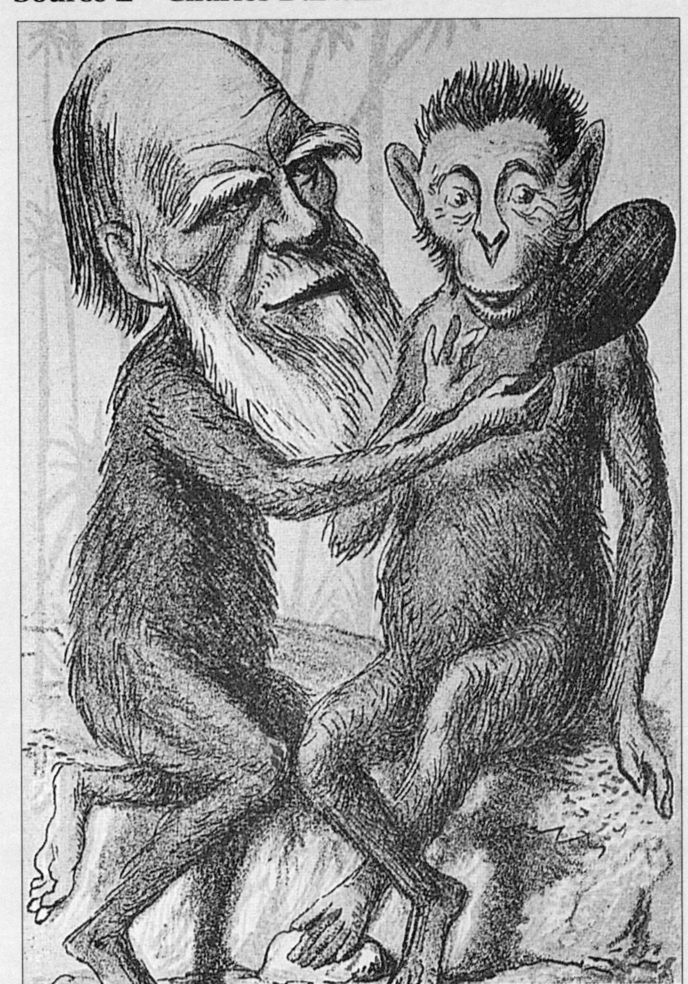

In 1859 Charles Darwin published his book 'The Origin of Species'. After lengthy research Darwin had concluded that human beings had evolved over millions of years from the same origin as apes. Many Christians were horrified by this book because the Bible said that human beings were God's special creation and that the world had been created in 6 days.

Source F

We look every Sunday at our well-filled churches and, seeing those who are present, we forget for the moment that many are absent. We forget that misery, sin, need of room, want of clothes, neglect or utter wretchedness are keeping many people away from our fellowship and cutting them off from civilisation and religion.

Samuel Wilberforce, 'A Charge Delivered to the Clergy of the Archdeaconry of Surrey', 1844

Source G

No one will ever understand Victorian England who does not appreciate that among highly civilised countries it was one of the most religious that the world has ever known.

R.C.K. Ensor, 'England 1870-1914', 1936

Activities

1. What is happening in Source A? What does this tell us about the Church of England in the 18th century? How far is this view supported by Source C?
2. 'The Church of England was failing in its duties.' Explain this statement using Sources B and F.
3. Do the figures in Source D prove or disprove the view expressed in Source G? Explain your answer.
4. What point is being made by the cartoon in Source E? What does it tell us about people's reactions to Darwin's 'The Origin of Species'?

Religion and reform

In the late 18th and early 19th century the number of people living in towns grew rapidly. The Religious Census of 1851 shows that the number of church-goers in towns was much smaller than in villages.

Some Christians - the Evangelicals - became worried about this. They were concerned about the decline of Christianity and shocked by the conditions in which people lived and worked. They supported reform in the hope that this would make Christianity popular again. Their special concern was the underprivileged sections of society.

Perhaps the best known Evangelical was Lord Shaftesbury. As an MP and later in the House of Lords Shaftesbury tried to get laws passed to improve working conditions, especially for women and children. He also worked outside Parliament trying to set up schools for poor children and to obtain better treatment for the mentally ill.

Source A **A shoe-shine boy points out Lord Shaftesbury**

Lord Shaftesbury became a symbol of hope to over-worked and underprivileged children. His efforts to stop small boys working down mines or up chimneys became well known in Britain and abroad.

Source B

I never went to a day school or a Sunday school. I got no clothes to go in. I cannot read or write. I never heard of Jesus Christ. I don't know what you mean by God. I never heard of Adam or know what you mean by Scripture. I have heard of the Bible but don't know what 'tis all about. I don't know what will happen to me hereafter if I am wicked. I have never been told. I don't know what Sunday is. There are 6 days in the week. I remember now that there is another day. Father gets drunk at Betty Bilsen's sometimes.

Replies to questions on religion by a boy coal miner, Parliamentary Papers, 1842

Source C **A Victorian schoolroom**

Christians were especially concerned about lack of education for poor people. Free schools - like this 'Ragged school' - were set up to teach the '3 Rs' (Reading, wRiting and aRithmetic) and lessons from the Bible. The Ragged Schools Union was set up in 1844 and Lord Shaftesbury became its President.

Source D

While women weep as they do now, I'll fight. While little children go hungry as they do now, I'll fight. While men go to prison, in and out, in and out, I'll fight. While there is a poor lost girl upon the street, I'll fight. While there remains one dark soul without the light of God, I'll fight - I'll fight to the very end.

William Booth, 'Darkest England and the Way Out', 1890

Source E A Salvation Army boys' hostel

The Salvation Army set up hostels for the homeless. Christians hoped that by providing food and shelter for the poorer sections of society, they would also be able to save their souls for God.

Source F

Evangelical religion is the chief cause of the improvement that is so obvious in the great masses of English society. We do not mean that great numbers are converted to God but we do mean that great numbers are under the direct influence of Christian religion.

From the 'Congregational Year Book', 1849

Source G The abolition of slavery

The Evangelical William Wilberforce was joined by Josiah Wedgwood, the pottery manufacturer, and other leading Christians in his campaign against slavery and the slave trade. Wedgwood produced thousands of medallions like the one above and gave them away.

Activities

1. Using Sources A, C, E and G make a list of the problems that Christians tried to solve and the ways in which they tried to solve them.
2. What does Source C tell us about Victorian attitudes to education? In what ways is your classroom different? Give reasons to explain this.
3. Look at Source B.
   a) What do you think would have concerned MPs most about the boy's answers? Why?
   b) What does this Source tell us about the importance of Christianity in Victorian education?
4. What do Sources D and F tell us about the aims of Evangelical Christians in the 19th century?

Punishment

Capital punishment was abolished in Britain in 1965. Since then nobody has been hanged for a crime. In 1750, however, over 200 crimes carried the death penalty. Punishment in the 18th century was based on the idea of revenge and deterrence (the hope that if one person was punished for a crime others would not dare to commit it). As a result, sentences were harsh and conditions in prison were appalling.

In the 19th century reformers argued that it was wrong to seek revenge. They said that the aim of punishment should be to help criminals not to commit crimes again. Many of these reformers were Christians. However, not all Christians agreed with their point of view. Today people continue to argue about the purpose of punishment.

Source A Corporal punishment

For minor offences people suffered corporal punishment (punishment which hurt them but did not endanger their lives). This often took place in public. People were encouraged to laugh at the criminals, shout abuse and throw things at them.

Source B Capital punishment

Until 1868 hangings often took place in public. Crowds gathered expecting a good day's entertainment. Seats with the best view were sold. Sometimes condemned criminals paid people in the crowd to pull on their legs when they were hanged. This broke their necks and prevented slow suffocation before death.

Source C The New Testament

You have learned that they were told 'an eye for an eye and a tooth for a tooth'. But what I tell you is this. Do not set yourself against the man who wrongs you. If someone slaps you on the right cheek, turn and offer him your left.

You have learned that they were told 'love your neighbour, hate your enemy'. But what I tell you is this. Love your enemies and pray for them. Only by doing so can you be children of your heavenly Father.

Matthew, 4: 38-9 and 43-5

Source D **Elizabeth Fry reading to prisoners in Newgate prison**

Elizabeth Fry, a Quaker, visited Newgate prison in 1813. Appalled by the conditions suffered by the women prisoners and their small children, she brought them mattresses and clothing and started sewing and Bible reading classes. She then spent much of her time campaigning for kinder treatment for all prisoners. She said, 'Punishment is not for revenge but to lessen crime and reform the criminal.'

Source E

In 1810 a Bill was brought forward cancelling an old law which made the theft of 5 shillings from a shop a capital offence. The Commons passed the Bill but the Lords threw it out. The Archbishop of Canterbury, the Bishop of London and five other Bishops voted against it.

Sir E.L. Woodward, 'The Age of Reform 1815-1870', 1938

Source F

Prisons are really meant to keep the masses in order and to be a terror to evil-doers. There must be solitude; coarse food; a dress of shame; hard, tiring, eternal labour; a planned and controlled exclusion of happiness and comfort.

An ideal prison according to the Reverend Sydney Smith (1771-1845)

Source G **A modern prison**

Many of the prisons in use today were built in Victorian times.

Activities

1. Look at Sources A and B. Why do you think punishment took place in public?
2. Look at Source C. Which of the sources on these pages show an 'eye for an eye' attitude and which show a 'love your enemy' attitude towards punishment? Explain your answers.
3. Using Sources D, E and F describe the different views that Christians had towards punishment. How can these views be explained?
4. Look at Source G. Would you say that progress has been made in punishment since the 19th century? Explain your answer.

Victorian values

Today when people use the term 'Victorian values' they are talking about the view of life held by Victorians from the middle classes. These people often had strict views about how people should behave. They argued that people should look after themselves and their family first and should not rely on outside help. They also argued that people should always avoid excess and live a life without 'sin' (especially in sexual matters).

Source A The ideal Victorian family

The ideal Victorian family consisted of two parents and several children. The whole family would gather together to sing hymns. The father, as head of the family, would always be obeyed. In public, the children would be 'seen but not heard'.

Source B

The men gathered every evening in the 'Waggon and Horses' and sipped half pints drop by drop (to make them last). None of them got drunk; they had not money enough. Yet the vicar preached against the pub, calling it a 'den of evil'. 'Tis a pity he can't come and see what it's like for himself', said an older man on the way home from church. 'Pity he can't mind his own business', added a younger one.

Flora Thompson, 'Lark Rise to Candleford', an account of life in the 1880s, 1973

Source C A Temperance Society banner

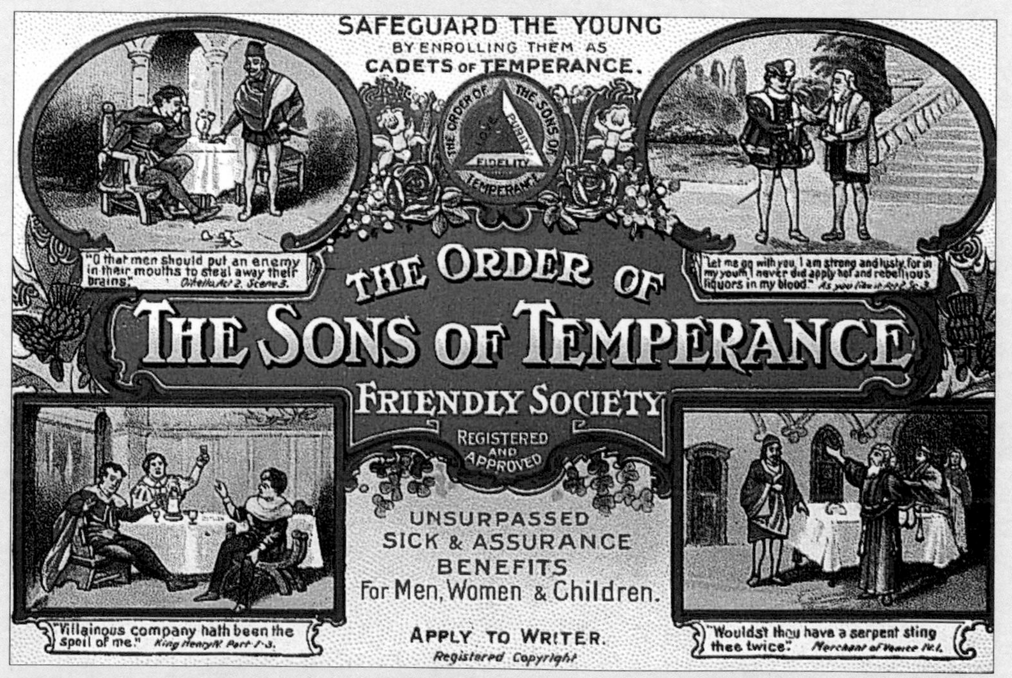

Middle class Victorians believed that alcoholic drink was the cause of many evils. Poverty, violence and crime were all blamed on alcohol. Many Temperance Societies grew up with the aim of persuading people (even children as young as ten years old) to pledge (promise) that they would never drink alcohol.

The 1883 FA Cup Final

In 1883 the FA Cup was won for the first time by a team of working class players from Blackburn. They beat the Cup-holders, the Old Etonians, 2-1 after extra time. Never again would a team made up of upper class players reach a Cup Final. The passage below describes the match and reactions to it.

After winning the FA Cup in 1882 (by beating Blackburn Rovers 1-0) the Old Etonians again reached the Final in 1883. On this occasion they encountered Rovers' main local rivals, Blackburn Olympic. 'The weather', reported *The Times*, 'was charming and the attendance (about 8,000) very large.' According to the *Eton College Chronicle*, the Old Etonians should have won easily. 'No one will deny that they were the better team of the two', it said, 'but it was their very confidence in this fact which probably lost them the match. Their play during the first part of the game was too casual and they should certainly have gained more than one goal while fresh.' Shortly after half time Arthur Dunn, the Old Etonian and England international (one of six internationals in their side), was forced to leave the field after being 'cannoned against and thrown' (according to *The Times*). By then, reported the *Athletic News*, 'a knocking out spirit seemed to have affected both teams'. Opinions differed on how this began. The *Manchester Guardian* said, 'For a long time the Etonians played pluckily and it is to be regretted that the Blackburn men fouled them so repeatedly'. The *Athletic News* disagreed, saying, 'In justice to the Blackburn lads who were playing on a strange ground and in front of a biased audience, it must be stated that the first signs of rough play came from their opponents'. Full time ended with the score 1-1. When extra time began, the Eton forwards were tired and a 'capital goal' gave Blackburn Olympic victory. Major Marindin, President of the FA, presented the cup and called for three cheers. 'Somewhat reluctant' applause followed from the spectators. But the cheers in Blackburn, Lancashire were anything but reluctant. Following the Final there was a period of football mania.

Christopher Andrew, '1883 Cup Final: Patricians v Plebeians', 1983

Recording reality

In the 18th and 19th centuries society was changing more rapidly and more dramatically than it had ever changed before. The expansion of industry and the Empire, the growth of towns and changes in technology created new sights, sounds and experiences for everyone. These new experiences affected the work of artists, musicians and writers. Some were enthusiastic about the changes whilst others used their work to campaign for reforms.

Source A Photography

Before photography was invented in the late 1830s the only way to record events was to write about them or to draw or paint them. Although the camera could be used to capture reality as it had never been seen before, this picture from 1900 shows that trick photography was soon discovered. Photography became a new art form.

Source B Literature

The rags of the dirty ballad-singer fluttered in the rich light that showed the jeweller's treasures. Pale, pinched-up faces hovered around the shop windows which were full of tempting food. Hungry eyes wandered over this abundance which was guarded by one thin sheet of brittle glass - an iron wall to them. Half-naked, shivering figures stopped to gaze at Chinese shawls and the golden stuffs from India. Life and death went hand in hand; wealth and poverty stood side by side.

Charles Dickens, 'Nicholas Nickleby', 1839

Source C Film poster for 'Nicholas Nickleby'

Like many of Charles Dickens' novels, 'Nicholas Nickleby' was first published as a monthly serial in a magazine. The first part appeared in April 1838 and it was not completed until 1839. Many of his novels dramatised the problems that people faced in 19th century Britain. The film was made in 1947, seventy seven years after Dickens died.

Source D Art and industry

The growth of industry presented totally new scenes for artists to capture. Some portrayed them very realistically. Others produced an idealised view.

Source E Music: the Last Night of the Proms

The Promenade concerts ('Proms') were first held in London in the 1890s. Their aim was to popularise classical music. Today the audience at the Last Night of the Proms dresses up, waves Union Jacks and joins in the singing of 'Rule Britannia' and 'Land of Hope and Glory'. This public display of patriotism stems from the time when Britain ruled a large Empire. The song 'Rule Britannia' ends, 'Rule Britannia! Britannia rules the waves! Britons never, never, never shall be slaves!'

Activities

1. Using the sources on these pages explain how changes in society affected: a) visual art; b) literature; c) music.
2. Using Sources A and D explain the problems that historians face when using photographs and paintings as historical source material.
3. Look at Sources B and C.
   a) Would you describe Source C as 'reliable' historical evidence? Explain your answer.
   b) If Dickens was alive today what subjects might he choose for his novels? Write an extract from a 'modern' Dickens novel.
4. Look at Source E. 'Rule Britannia' has been popular since it was written in 1740. Why do you think this is so?

Escaping from reality

Although the great changes in society affected everyone, some people aimed to escape reality in their leisure time. The arts provided the means to do this. Artists sometimes ignored the changes around them and chose instead to paint imaginary or historical scenes. Writers did not always write about the real world. They invented worlds of fantasy and adventure.

During the 19th century the number of people who learned to read increased. As the number of readers grew so did the variety of reading material. For example, throughout the 19th century comics were very popular with young and older people alike. Unlike modern comics, 19th century comics contained just one or two illustrations. Each issue described an adventure which was continued the next week.

Source A A film poster for 'Frankenstein'

The film 'Frankenstein' (made in 1931) was based on a book written by Mary Shelley in 1816. In the story, Dr Frankenstein discovers the secret of bringing dead flesh back to life and uses this secret to create a monster. The idea of 'science gone mad' was new and many later works of Science Fiction are based on it.

Source B 'The Lady of Shalott' by J. W. Waterhouse, a 'Pre-Raphaelite'

The 'Pre-Raphaelites' (a group of painters and writers) emphasised the values of pre-industrial Britain - a mythical land full of brave knights, contented peasants and romantic adventure. Many of their paintings were based on ancient legends. The story of King Arthur with its tales of knightly chivalry was especially popular.

Source C Comics

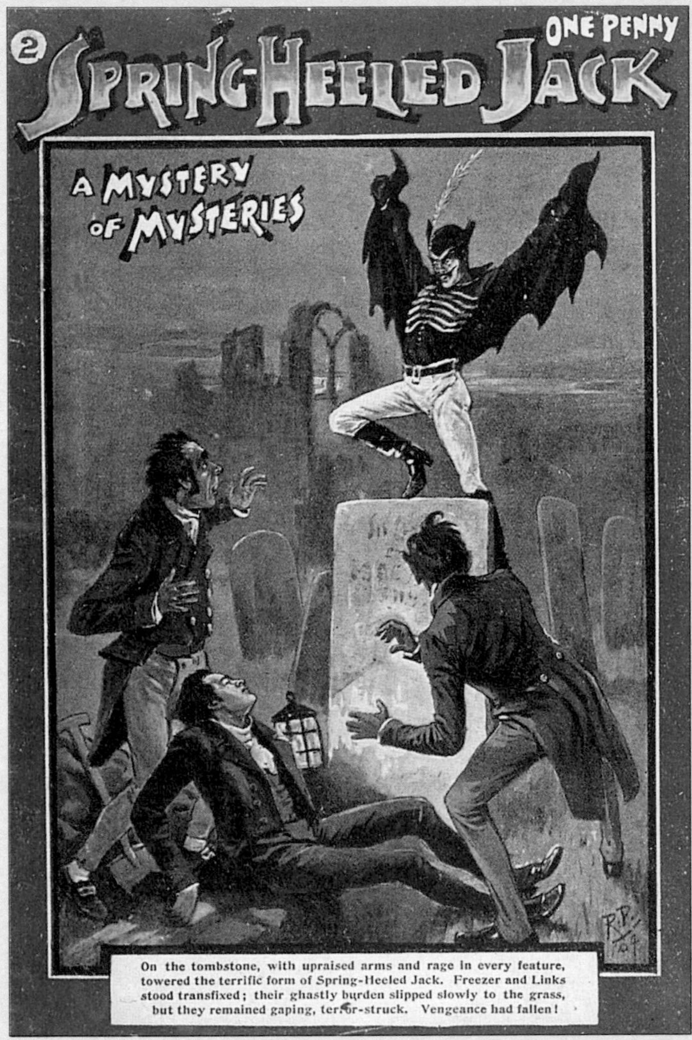

Weekly comics became known as 'penny dreadfuls'. The front cover usually contained an illustration of the adventure which was described inside. The adventures of 'Spring-Heeled Jack' were especially popular in the 1870s.

Source D 'The War of the Worlds'

The year is 1894 and the Martians have landed in London...

Saturday lives in my memory as a day of suspense. I had slept but little and rose early. The milkman came as usual. I heard the rattle of his chariot and I went round to the side gate to ask the latest news. He told me that during the night the Martians had been surrounded by troops and that guns were expected. Then a familiar reassuring note, I heard a train running towards Woking. 'They aren't to be killed', said the milkman, 'if it can possibly be avoided.'

I saw my neighbour and chatted to him. My neighbour was of the opinion that the troops would be able to capture or destroy the Martians during the day.

H.G. Wells, 'The War of the Worlds', a serial in 'Pearson's Magazine', 1897

Source E Excerpt from a 'penny dreadful'

'Whatever unhappy wretch reads these lines may bid goodbye to the world and all hope, for he is a doomed man! He will never emerge from these vaults with life, for there is a secret connected with them so awful and so hideous that to write it makes one's blood curdle and the flesh creep upon your bones. The secret is this - and you may be assured, whoever is reading these lines, that I write the truth and it would be impossible to make the awful truth worse by exaggeration...' The message on the wall broke off at this point.

T. Peckett Prest, 'The String of Pearls', 1840

Activities

1. Look at Sources A and D.
   a) Why do you think that Science Fiction was first written in the 19th century?
   b) *Frankenstein* and *The War of the Worlds* became very popular. Why do you think this was so?
2. Why do you think 'Pre-Raphaelite' artists chose to paint pictures like that in Source B? What does this tell us about their attitude to the world they lived in?
3. Look at Sources C and E.
   a) Why do you think comics were called 'penny dreadfuls'?
   b) Write a story to go with Source C or complete the story in Source E.
4. Choose any two sources on these pages and explain how useful they are to someone studying British history between 1750 and 1900.

Leisure: holidays, sport & music

Where did you spend your holidays last year? At home? At the seaside? Or, did you fly off to some far corner of the world? The idea that most people should be able to spend time away on holiday is fairly new. It resulted from different working patterns and the new forms of transport that developed in the 19th century.

Rich people had always enjoyed plenty of leisure time. It was usual for the children of rich families to spend six months doing the 'Grand Tour of Europe' after leaving school, for example. But most people had neither the time nor the money to go on holiday. This only began to change with the reform of working conditions, improving standards of living and cheap transport.

Holidays were not the only result of these changes. Greater leisure time also meant the possibility of enjoying sport and other activities.

Source A The impact of railways

LANCASHIRE & YORKSHIRE RAILWAY

FROM THE GLOOM OF THE TOWN
TO THE SUNNY SOUTH COAST

ENGLISH CHANNEL

CHEAP FARES AND EXPRESS SERVICES TO THE SOUTH COAST HOLIDAY RESORTS
APPLY AT THE STATIONS & TOWN AGENCIES FOR FULL PARTICULARS

The growth of the railways meant that people were able to travel away from towns to the countryside or to the seaside. One of the first people to recognise the opportunity for tourism was Thomas Cook. In 1841 he said, 'We must have railways for the millions.' He organised some of the first rail trips to the seaside.

Source B Margate in the 19th century

By the end of the 19th century millions of people had been to the seaside for their holidays. The 'Bank Holiday Act' of 1871 made certain days official holidays. Townspeople saved up all year to be able to spend the bank holiday at the seaside. Many coastal towns, such as Margate and Blackpool, owed their growth to the new tourist industry. Hotels, amusement arcades and piers were built. Donkeys and bathing machines (to allow people to bathe in private) were hired out, food was sold and people could watch Punch and Judy shows.

Source C A cricket match between Sussex and Kent

Ease of travel and greater leisure time encouraged the growth of organised nation-wide sport in the late 19th century. The Focus shows that from the 1880s football became increasingly popular with ordinary people. The FA Cup began in 1871 and the Football League was founded with 12 clubs in 1888. Cricket was also a popular pastime. Many village leagues were set up. The County Championship started in 1873. The first Test Match against Australia was played in Melbourne in 1877. Australia won.

Source D The Music Hall

The 1890s has been described as the 'golden age of the English Music Hall'. Singers, dancers, comedians and even brass bands performed in the Music Halls. Many of the performers became household names.

Source E

The two Music Halls in the town are always full. The front row of the gallery generally consists of small children who eagerly follow every detail of the entertainment. Workmen can be seen in the orchestra stalls. There are more men than women. Many of the women have their babies in their arms. There is no doubt that they come out looking pleased and brightened up.

Lady Florence Bell, 'At the Works', 1907

Activities

1. It is 1875 and you have just been on holiday to the seaside for the first time. Describe your holiday using Sources A and B.
2. Look at Source C. What does this Source tell you about cricket in the 19th century? What has changed and what has remained the same?
3. Look at Sources D and E. Why do you think the Music Hall was popular in the 19th century? Why do you think Music Halls no longer exist?
4. 'In the late 19th century popular culture in Britain was changing.' Explain this statement using the sources on these pages.

The Great Exhibition

In 1851 Queen Victoria opened an exhibition of the 'Works of Industry of All Nations' - the first modern international exhibition ever to be held. The 'Great Exhibition' was the idea of her husband, Prince Albert. Its aim was not just to celebrate the progress made in arts and science but also to show off Britain's technological and cultural achievements. A massive glass building - the Crystal Palace - was built in Hyde Park to house the exhibits. Inside, there were 7,381 British exhibitors and 6,556 from other countries. Visitors came from all over Britain and from abroad. In total there were 6,039,195 visitors. The profits from the exhibition were used to buy land in South Kensington. The Natural History Museum, the Science Museum and the Victoria and Albert Museum now stand on this land.

Source A The Crystal Palace

The idea of constructing a large building entirely out of glass and iron was a new concept in architecture. These materials were used so that the Crystal Palace could be dismantled and rebuilt when the exhibition was over. The building was over 600 metres long - three times the length of St Paul's cathedral. It was put up in six months. After the exhibition it was moved to a site in South London where it stood until 1936 when it burned down.

Source B The Indian room at the Great Exhibition

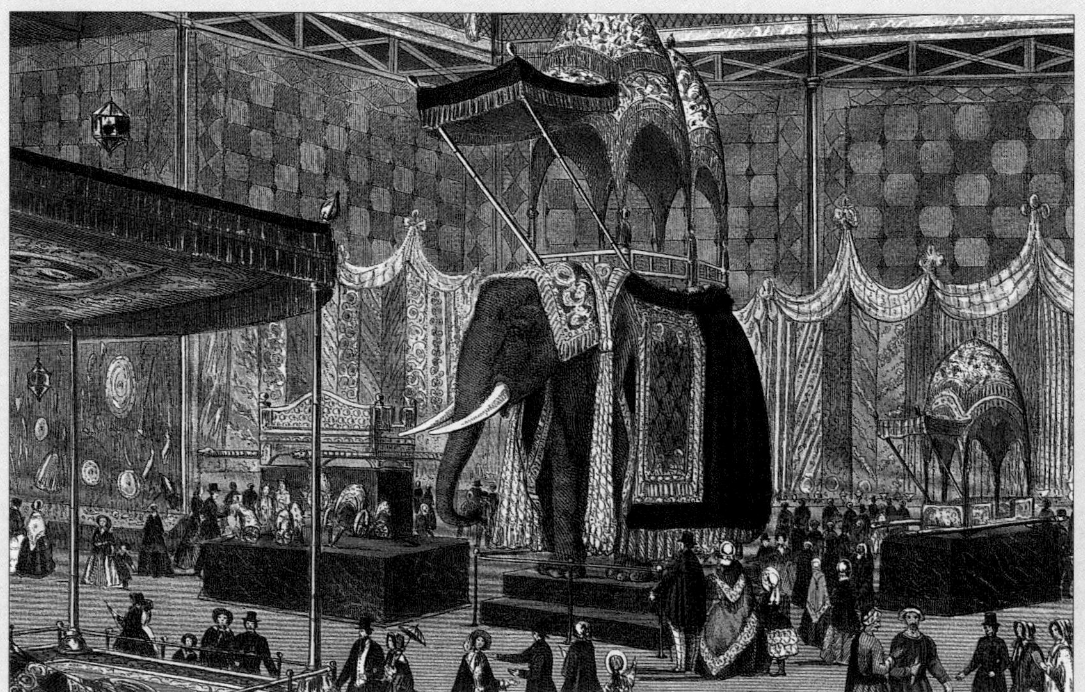

Few of the British visitors knew much about the British Empire. The exhibition included displays from the colonies, such as India.
The British displays contained many of the most up-to-date machines available at the time - for example, a printing press which printed 100,000 sheets of newspaper per hour and a full-size steam train. Works of art included a 7 metre high statue of Queen Victoria.

Source C Calcutta, India, c.1900

One of the aims of the Great Exhibition was to show off just how 'modern' and 'advanced' Britain was. British culture had a great influence on the wider world, especially on the British colonies.

Source D A letter to the King of Prussia (Germany)

Mathematicians have calculated that the Crystal Palace will blow down in the first gale. Engineers calculate that the galleries will crash in and destroy the visitors. Economists have predicted a scarcity of food in London owing to the vast number of visitors that are expected. Doctors say that because so many races will come into contact with each other, the plague of the Middle Ages will make its appearance as it did after the Crusades. Moralists predict that England will be infected by all the evils of the civilised and uncivilised world. Theologians say that the exhibition will draw upon it the vengeance of an offended God. But I believe we will succeed.

Prince Albert, 1851

Checklist

- Changes in society between 1750 and 1900 affected the arts. Real life was portrayed in the arts but there was also a desire to escape from reality.
- There was an increase in organised leisure activities in the late 19th century.
- The Great Exhibition, held in 1851, celebrated Britain's technological and cultural achievements. British culture made a big impact on the wider world.

Activities

1. Many of the British visitors to the Great Exhibition had never left their home town before. Suppose that you had been one of them. Using Sources A and B, write a diary which describes your reactions to what you saw.
2. Look at Source C. Make a list of all the examples of British influence that you can see.
3. What does Source D tell us about the problems faced by Prince Albert when he tried to organise the Great Exhibition?
4. If you were asked to design an exhibition today which celebrated the modern age, what would it be like? Make a presentation which includes a description of the building for the exhibition and the kind of exhibits you would include.

Acknowledgements

Cover photograph Mansell collection

Cover design Caroline Waring-Collins (Waring Collins Partnership)

Illustrations Caroline Waring-Collins (Waring Collins Partnership)

Page design Andrew Allen

Readers Lisa Fabry and Mike Haralambos

Picture credits

Ashmolean Museum, Oxford 64 (all); Author's Collection 29; BFI Stills, Posters and Designs 88(b), 90(t); Bridgeman Art Library 7(bl), 11(b), 13(t), 15, 20, 22(b), 23, 25, 33, 35, 42(b), 51, 71, 79, 80(t), 82(b), 89(t), 92(b); British Library 61(b); Eversley Photography 80(b); Eye Ubiquitous 75(b); The Fotomas Index 67(b), 93(t); Roy Gower 24(r); Mike Henfield 50(tl); Hulton Deutsch 21(b), 28(b), 39(t), 42(t), 83(t); Institute of Agricultural History 11(t); Kelham Island Museum, Sheffield 27(t), 27(b); Mansell Collection, 13(br), 21(t), 43, 47, 48, 52, 57(all), 59, 62(b), 65, 77, 78(t), 94(b); Mary Evans Picture Library 30, 34, 44(t), 45, 50(br), 53(t), 55, 58(b), 69, 72(r), 87, 91, 92(t), 94(t), 95; Performing Arts Library 89(b); Peter Newark's Historical Pictures 7(tl), 16, 40(b), 44(b), 70(t), 73(r), 74, 81(t); Picturepoint 4, 6(t), 6(m), 6(b), 7(tr), 7(br), 9, 12, 39b), 40(t), 46(l), 62(t), 84(b), 85; Picturesport Associates 86(all); Royal Doulton Limited 31; Rex Features 56(t), 56(m); Sefton Photo Library 24(l), 49(t), 53(b); Topham Picture Source 5(t), 5(b), 18, 32(l), 32(r), 46(r), 54, 56(b), 63, 67(t), 70(b), 73(l), 83(b); The Wedgwood Museum 22(t), 81(b).

Every effort has been made to locate the copyright owners of material used in this book. Any omissions brought to our attention are regretted and will be credited in subsequent printings.

Causeway Press Ltd
PO Box 13, Ormskirk, Lancashire L39 5HP

1st impression 1992, reprinted 1994, 1996, 1999

British Library Cataloguing in Publication Data – a catalogue record for this book is available from the British Library

ISBN 0 946183 96 1

Typesetting by John A. Collins, (Waring Collins Partnership), Ormskirk, Lancashire L39 1QR
Printed and bound by Cambus Litho Ltd, East Kilbride